John Anderson

History of the Belfast Library and Society for Promoting Knowledge

Commonly known as the Linen Hall Library, chiefly taken from the minutes of the

society, and published in connection with the centenary celebration in 1888

John Anderson

History of the Belfast Library and Society for Promoting Knowledge
*Commonly known as the Linen Hall Library, chiefly taken from the minutes of the society, and
published in connection with the centenary celebration in 1888*

ISBN/EAN: 9783337248673

Printed in Europe, USA, Canada, Australia, Japan

Cover: Foto ©ninafisch / pixelio.de

More available books at **www.hansebooks.com**

History of
The Linen Hall Library.

LINEN HALL LIBRARY, BELFAST, 1888.

HISTORY

OF

The Belfast Library and Society for Promoting Knowledge,

COMMONLY KNOWN AS

THE LINEN HALL LIBRARY,

Chiefly taken from the Minutes of the Society,

AND PUBLISHED IN CONNECTION WITH

THE CENTENARY CELEBRATION

in 1888.

By JOHN ANDERSON.
Hon. Secretary.

Belfast

M'CAW, STEVENSON & ORR, LINENHALL WORKS.

1888.

Preface.

IN presenting the following short History of the rise and progress of the Linen Hall Library, the author feels that some apology is due for the imperfections of his work. When the suggestion was made to commemorate the Centenary of the Library by the publication of an historical sketch, he, amongst others, highly approved of the proposal. But this was under the impression that someone else would be found to undertake the work of compilation and preparation. As, however, none of the gentlemen to whom application was made could see their way to do so, the author was, somewhat reluctantly, induced to accept the kind invitation of his colleagues to undertake a task which he felt conscious might have been better accomplished by another.

Now that the work, such as it is, is completed, he is free to admit that whatever labour its preparation may have cost him has been amply repaid by the pleasure and gratification he has received in tracing the history of one of the most useful institutions of the town, and in having this opportunity of commemorating the noble and generous efforts of the band of men whom we are proud to regard as our predecessors, to whose energy and wisdom the present prosperity of the Library is chiefly due.

The History, which is principally drawn from the Minute Books of the Society, will show from what small beginnings the present Library sprung; and, as we follow its career down through the century, it presents a record of varied progress, until the close of the present Centennial year, when it claims to stand at a point of higher prosperity than it has ever before reached.

Apart from its interest as the history of one of our venerable institutions, this record can hardly fail to throw some light on the history and progress of Belfast during the past century. The interests of the Society appear to have been always in the hands of many of the ablest and most public-spirited of our fellow-citizens; and if we had nothing here but the list of names of those associated from time to time with this Society, the muster-roll would be found to include many of those to whom Belfast is indebted for its present religious, intellectual, and material prosperity.

The author's original intention had been to prefix to this History a sketch of the state of the town and neighbourhood at the eventful period in which the Society was first established. But it was thought better to confine the work within its proper limits, and only remind the reader, as occasion arose, of the stirring events in which many of its early supporters were themselves participators.

The first part of the History, down to 1800, describing the origin and early proceedings of the Society, anterior to its settlement in the Linen Hall, has been arranged in short chapters, dealing with the various subjects connected with that period. The second part has been arranged in the form of annals, presenting under each year the principal matters recorded in the Minutes. Lists of members have been given at various periods of the Society's history, and a large number of personal notes have been added, although it has been deemed better not to continue these beyond a date where they relate to individuals now living. In the Appendix will be found a considerable amount of statistical and other information which could not be conveniently embodied in the text.

In conclusion, the author begs to tender his sincere thanks to those who have assisted him in his labours; and trusts that the possession of this book by the members of the Society whose history it commemorates may be valued, not for its own merits, but as a record of one of the best and most successful enterprises of our loyal and progressive town.

JOHN ANDERSON.

Linen Hall Library,
    Belfast, *13th May*, 1888.

Contents.

PART I.

PART II.

APPENDICES.

Illustrations.

PART I.

EARLY HISTORY OF THE SOCIETY,
1788-1800.

I.

The Belfast Reading Society: Its Formation and Search for Premises.

THE BELFAST READING SOCIETY—of which "the Belfast Library and Society for Promoting Knowledge" is the outcome—was established on the 13th of May, 1788. Beyond this bare fact, appended to a signed copy of the original rules, the Minutes afford no information as to the circumstances under which the Society originated, or the object of its operations. It is not, indeed, until four years later that we find a distinct statement on the records of the objects and aims of the original founders. "The great and first object of the Society," it is here stated, "is to form a "Library, which should remain *for ever* the sole and *undivided* property of the whole "Society;" and, subsequently, we find that "the object of this Society is the collection "of an extensive Library, Philosophical Apparatus, and such productions of Nature and "Art as tend to improve the mind, and excite a spirit of general enquiry."

There is little doubt that these principles, though not formally recorded at the time, actuated the founders in establishing the Belfast Reading Society ; and it will be interesting, as forming the first entry in the records, to reproduce here the original rules, with the names appended.

13th May, 1788.   Rule 1. That the mode of admitting members shall be by ballot, six black beans excluding.

2nd. That every candidate for admittance must be known to one or more of the regular members, or recommended by some person in whom the Society can place confidence, and be proposed one month previous to admittance.

3rd. That each member shall pay monthly the sum of one shilling brittish, as long as the Society shall deem it necessary.

4th. That the sum to be paid by members who shall be admitted one year or upwards after the commencement of the Society, shall be regulated from time to time by a majority of the Society.

13th May, 1788.

5th. That no member shall have the use of any book longer than fourteen days, if called for by any other member of the Society.

6th. That no member shall be at liberty to lend out of his house or family any book or books the property of the Society, and for every such offence when detected, shall be fined Five british shillings, besides being accountable for whatever Injury such book or books may thereby have received.

7th. That each mem. shall sign an obligation to pay *the first* the first cost or value of of any book he may Injure, lose, or not return to the Society, and the full value of any Set he may render Incomplete *by so doing*.

8th. That any member who does not pay his monthly subscription or cause it to be paid on the day appointed for that purpose shal be fined the sum of three pence. No excuse for failure will be admitted.

9th. That any member who shall be three months in arrears to the Society will not be supplyed with any books from the library untill arrears and fines are paid up.

10th. That any member who shall be in arrears to the Society one year's subscription or Twelve shillings brittish shall thereby forfeit his property in the library and privilege in the Society and cannot be restored to either without producing satisfactory reasons to the Committee and paying his arrears.

11th. That the Committee shall consist of (five) members who shall be chosen by ballot, who shall choose and purchase the books for the use of the Society, specify the fines and take such steps as may be proper and necessary to enforce obedience to and due observance of the regulations, who shall lay their transactions, state of the accounts and library *quarterly* before a meeting of the Society at which meeting the Committee shall be chosen.

12th. It being absolutely necessary that the Committee and Sec^y should attend the different meetings of the Society, a *fine* of one british shilling shall be paid by any member thereof who shall be absent and a fine of sixpence british on not appearing till half an hour after the hour of meeting.

13th. That any member shall have power to sell or bequeath his property in the Lib^y

14th. That if upon enquiry it shall appear that any member died without selling or bequeathing his property in the library, said property shall be transferable to the heir of the deceased member, with this proviso that said heir or person to whom said property may be sold or bequeathed shall be admitted by the same mode and on the same principles as other members are, and if said heir or purchaser be rejected by the Society they have a liberty of transferring their property ad Infinitum untill there is a person proposed considered as Eligible to be admitted as a member in the Society.

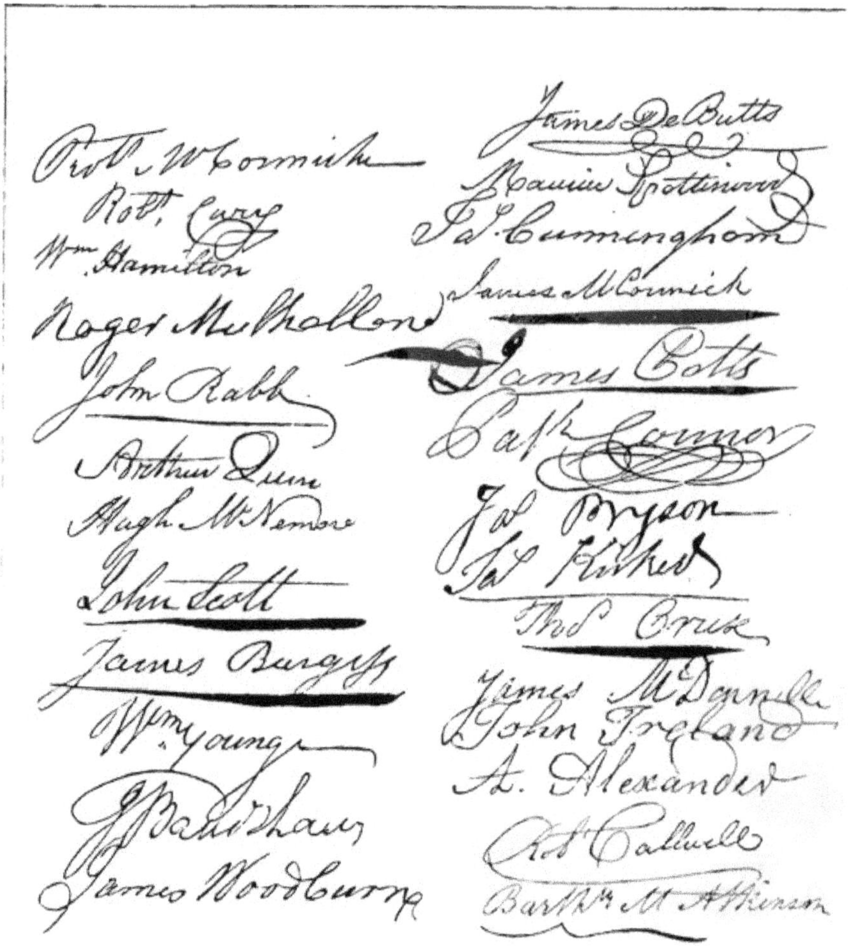

The Autograph Signatures in Fac-simile c

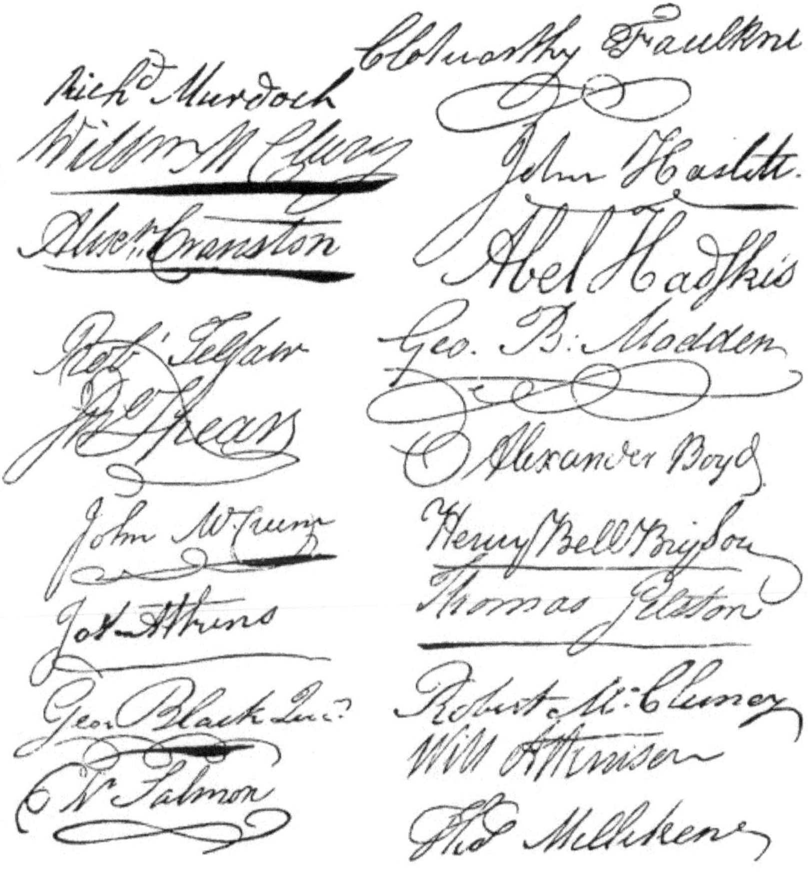

the early Members who signed the Roll.

13th May, 1788.

15th. That each member shall declare his approbation and bind himself to the strict and faithfull observance of these regulations by subscribing his name.

BELFAST, *13th May*, 1788.

*Robt. M'Cormick	*James De Butts	John Spears
*Robt. Cary	*Maurice Spottiswood	John M'Crum
*Wm. Hamilton	*Jas. Cunningham	James Atkins
*Roger Mulholland	*James M'Cormick	Geo. Black, Jur.
*John Rabb	*James Potts	Christopher Salmon
*Arthur Quin	*Patk. Connor	Clotworthy Faulkner
*Hugh M'Nemara	*Thos. Cruse	John Haslett
John Scott	*James M'Donnell	Abel Hadskis
*James Burgess	A. Alexander	Geo. F. Madden
Wm. Young	Robt. Callwell	Alexander Boyd
J. Bradshaw	Barthw. M. Atkinson	Henry Bell Bryson
*James Woodburn	*Richd. Murdock	Thomas Gelston
Jas. Bryson	Willm. M'Cleery	Robert M'Cluney
Jas. Kirker	Alexr. Cranston	Will. Atkinson
John Ireland	Rob. Telfair	Thos. Milliken

The eighteen names marked with an asterisk in the foregoing list appear to be those of the original founders of the Society. The minutes make no record of their election, whereas the others appear to have been duly elected in accordance with the rules, during and after the year 1791.[1] The autograph signatures of the early members who subscribed are given on the accompanying fac-simile.

The early proceedings of the Society are enveloped in mystery. No minutes appear to have been kept until the end of 1791. Whether in the interval the progress of the undertaking had been suspended, or whether the beginnings of the library had been made, meetings held, and fresh members elected, we have no means of ascertaining.

Nor are we informed as to the particular place, if any, in which, during the first three years of its existence, the Society had its habitation. The early minutes are, indeed, largely occupied with a record of the efforts to procure suitable premises. A brief account of the migrations which ultimately ended in the satisfactory location of the Society at the White Linen Hall, will not be without interest here.

It would appear from the following minute, dated 4th August, 1792, that the first premises, wherever they were, were not considered satisfactory.

4th Aug., 1792.   Resolved—That the Secretary call a Meeting of Committee to consider the propriety of an application to the Committee of the Belfast Charitable Society for the use of the Great Room in the Poor House for our Library, and the best means of carrying the measure into effect.

(1). The name of Æneas Lamont, though not among the signatories, should be added to those of the original members; and appears in the early Minutes as such. Mr. Lamont was uncle to Mr. W. S. Lamont, of Dromore, Co. Down.

But although the General Board granted the " Bail Room" to the Society at a nominal rent, the books and other property were not removed there, because, on further consideration, the premises were not considered sufficiently central.

After an application in November, 1792, for a room at the Linen Hall, which at the time appears to have had no result, a Committee was appointed to "look out for a place "suitable for the accommodation and purposes of the library," with power " to offer such "terms on behalf of the Society as may not injure the funds of the Society."

On the 14th of the same month (November) the Committee report—

14th Nov., 1792.   That they have found a house in Factory Row[1] in their opinion perfectly adapted for a repository for the Library and habitation for the Librarian, being 20 feet in front, 3 stories high, new and well-finished. A lease of fifty years or thereabouts may be had at the sum of £24 ℔ ann., which your Committee think remarkably cheap.

The Committee, therefore, sanctioned the taking of this house, on the longest lease possible, at the rent named. But the negotiations appear to have come to nothing.

Overtures were again made to the Linen Hall ; and the Committee of Selection was empowered "to go as far as £20 per annum for the rent of the front room." Once more, however, the business fell through, and on the 2nd January, 1793, it was resolved—

2nd Jan., 1793.   That it be recommended to the Society immediately to adopt a plan for enabling themselves to build a house convenient for all their purposes, and that they appoint a Committee of five to draw up a plan for that purpose.

This recommendation was adopted, and a Committee appointed to carry it out, consisting of Messrs. Robert Bradshaw, William Sinclaire, John Holmes, and Drs. White and M'Donnell.

At a subsequent meeting, it was decided that the question of the securing of premises was urgent, and it was resolved—

31st Jan., 1793.   That in the present situation of affairs, it would be a prudent measure to hire Mr. Cary's large Room, to hold the Books and receive the Meetings of the Committee, until the Society shall be accommodated with a house.

A sub-committee was appointed to treat with Mr. Cary—the situation of whose house is not stated—and at a General Meeting of the Society, on the 2nd of March, it was resolved—

2nd Mar., 1793.   That the offer made by Mr. Cary in his letter, of which the following is a copy, be acceded to, with this proviso—That the Society be at liberty to withdraw the Books, &c., at a quarter of a year's notice, and that Mr. Cary fits up his large Room with shelves, &c., for the arrangement of the books :—

(t). Now Derry Street.

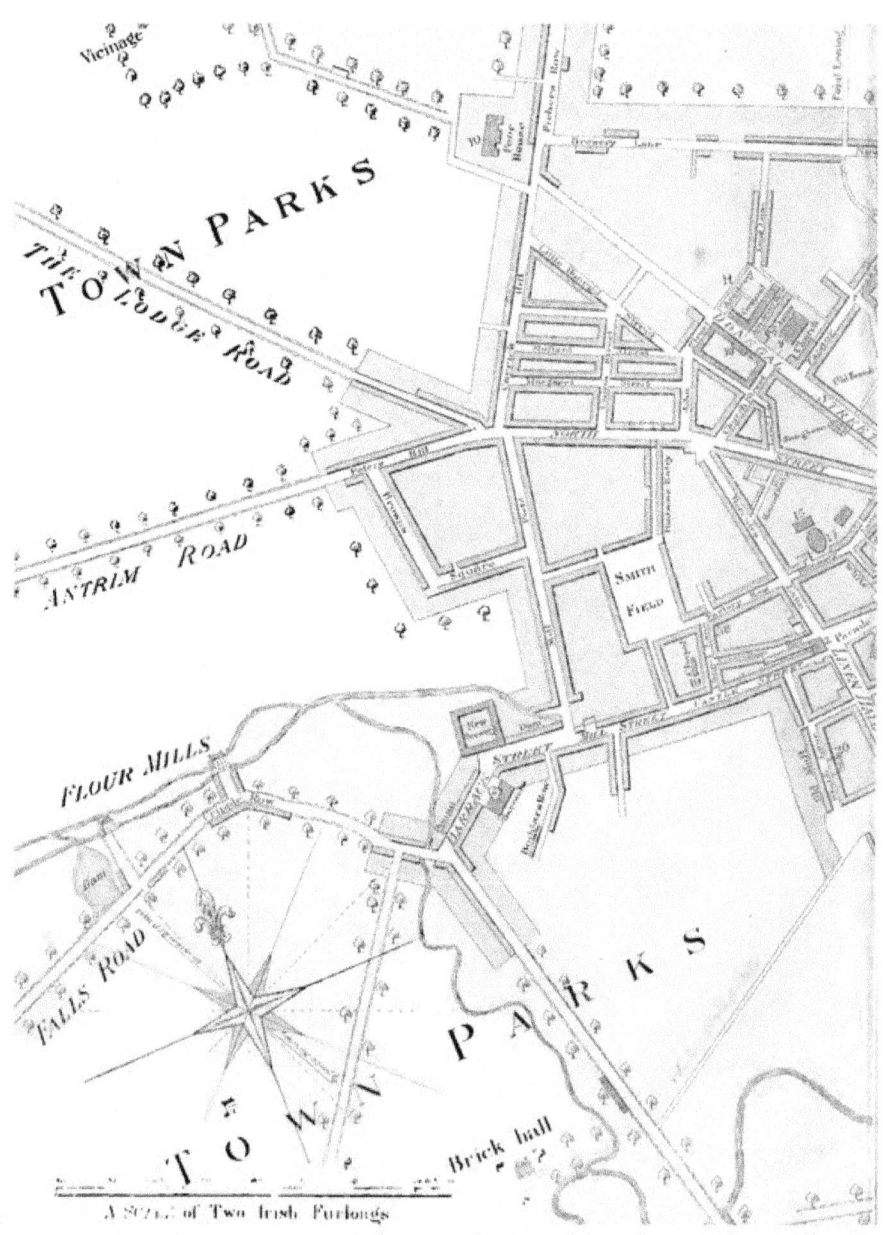

Vicinage

T O W N   P A R K S

THE LODGE ROAD

TO

ANTRIM   ROAD

FLOUR MILLS

FALLS ROAD

SMITH
FIELD

T   O   W   N   P   A   R   K   S

Brick hill

A SCALE of Two Irish Furlongs

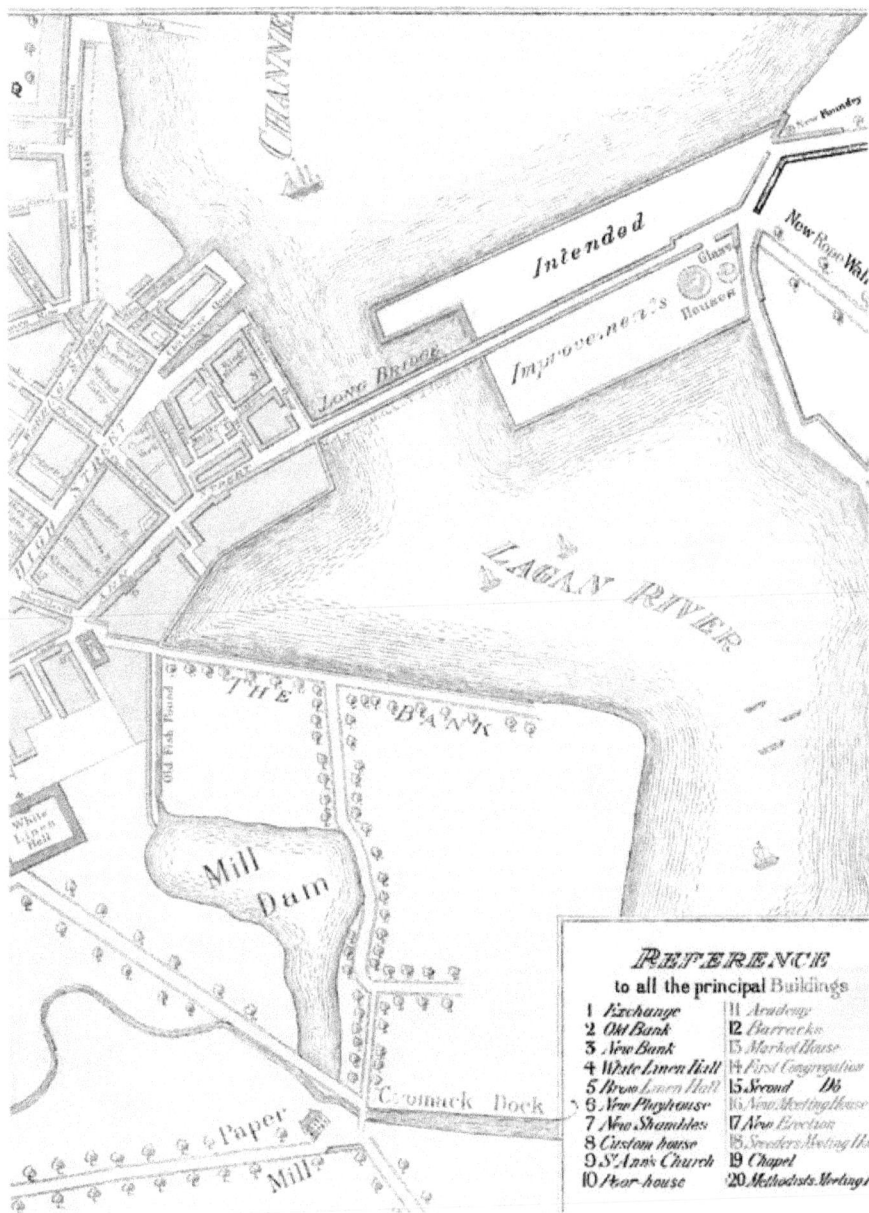

CHANNEL

New Foundry

Intended

Improvements

Glass Houses

New Rope Walk

Long Bridge

LAGAN RIVER

THE BANK

Old Fish Pound

White Linen Hall

Mill Dam

Cromac Dock

Paper

Mill

2nd Mar., 1793.

"To WILLIAM CLARKE and GEORGE B. MADDEN, Esqrs.

"GENTLEMEN—The terms I mean to keep the books on, and what I wish you
"would make known to the Society this night, is—For Librarian, 20 guineas l⁹ year,
"commencing the 1st Feb. last; and for the use of my room for Committee Meetings,
"5 guineas l⁹ year. If these terms are acceptable to the Society, they shall be so to,
"gentlemen, your very humble servant,　　"ROBERT CARY.

"Belfast, 2nd March, 1793."

This arrangement only lasted a year ; and we find that as early as April, in the same
year, the Committee were once more on the look-out for better quarters. Their attention
was called to "the Building, formerly the Methodist Meeting House (now vacant)[1] ; "
but, after inspection, they reported the premises unsuitable, on account of its situation
and present state, and "not an object worthy of the Society's attention."

At the commencement of 1794, the office of Librarian having become vacant, the
Committee reported—

6th Jan., 1794.　　That, agreeably to the direction of the Society to report our opinion
relative to a house for the Library, we report that the house at present in
the possession of Robert Telfair is the best calculated for the purpose of
any that has yet been proposed to our consideration, which opinion we
found on the following reasons—viz. :—The Society may in it be accomo-
dated with two Rooms, 19 feet by 12 each, beside a closet for the
Museum. The situation is in the highest degree eligible, being in the
most central part of the town, within two doors of the Market House, and
the character of the proprietor being unobjectionable. We conceive it an
additional argument in favour of the house that he has proposed himself
as a person qualified for the office of Librarian.

But at a General Meeting of the Society, held two days later, the choice for Librarian
fell upon Mr. Thomas Russell, and it was at the same time decided that "the expense
"attending a house for the Library, Museum, &c., and the Librarian's salary, should not
"exceed £30 per annum."

Mr. Russell was now entrusted with the duty of seeking a suitable place, and on
February 27th reported that he had engaged rooms for the Library in Ann Street, nearly
opposite the Discount Office.

It was thereupon resolved—

27th Feb., 1794.　　That Mr. Russell be authorized and requested to prepare one of the
rooms for the reception of the Books at the expence of the Society.

Here we have the first definite indication of the premises in which the Books were
kept. As the Discount Office (or Bank, as it is called) is shown on the accompanying
Map of Belfast, 1792, the situation of the Library may easily be determined.

The Library remained at Ann Street for several years, although in all respects the
premises do not appear to have given satisfaction.

(1). This Meeting House was in Fountain Street, nearly opposite to College Street.

In September, 1799, however, steps were again taken towards a removal, and it was resolved—

5th Sept., 1799.   That the situation of the house where the Library is kept is inconvenient and disagreeable to most of the members. That a committee be appointed to find a house which may answer for keeping the Library, and may be more agreeably situate than the present, provided the Rent do not exceed what is paid for the present house.

A few days later the Committee reported that they had taken a house in Donegall Street, at £25 per annum, and that they had sub-let two rooms in it to Mr. Gilbert M'Ilveen at £8 a year.[1] This house was on the site now occupied by the Northern Counties Railway as a parcels office.

After two years at Donegall Street a further removal was determined upon. In April, 1801, an offer of premises from a Mr. Carson was declined, but it was resolved to invite the Society to consider the propriety of removing to another house.

No action appears to have been taken till November, when it was reported—

6th Nov., 1801.   That the Subscribers of the Linen Hall have made an offer to the Society of the Room over the central part of the Hall for the Library free of all expence.

This generous offer was gladly accepted, and on the 10th it was decided to transfer the Library accordingly, and resolved—

10th Nov., 1801.   That the thanks of this Society be returned to the Subscribers of the White Linen Hall, and that it be published once in the "Belfast News-Letter."

A committee was appointed to carry out the arrangement for the transfer of the Society's property. This appears to have occupied a considerable time, as it was not till the 27th May, 1802, that the Society held its first meeting in the White Linen Hall, in which place its head-quarters have continued to the present time.

Since this memorable epoch in the history of the Society, it has been found necessary from time to time to apply to the Proprietors of the Linen Hall for additional accommodation, and it is with the greatest respect and gratitude that the Society record that such applications have never been met with a refusal.

II.

Notes of the Early Proceedings of the Society.

HAVING briefly noted the circumstances under which the Society, thirteen years after its establishment, happily found a permanent habitation in the Linen Hall, and before proceeding to give an account of the formation of the Library and scientific collections there deposited, it will be of interest to offer a few notes upon the proceedings and management of the Society during the early unsettled years of its career.

(1). As to the taxes imposed at that time, it appears by the accounts that Mr. M'Ilveen's proportion of the Hearth and Window Tax for these rooms amounted to £1 14s 1½d per annum. For the Ann Street premises the Society had paid for the same taxes £4 6s 11d.

Reference has already been made to an important early Minute, which states the aims and objects of the Belfast Reading Society in the following precise terms :—

10th July, 1792. The great and first object of this Society being to form a Library, which should remain *for ever* the sole and *undivided* property of the whole Society—in order to do away with the possibility of *any part* of the Society, *however great their majority*, at any future time disposing of, or dividing, the books contrary to the principles on which the Society was originally formed—it was unanimously resolved—

That this Society cannot dissolve themselves, or proceed to a division or disposal of the Library, unless by an *unanimous vote* of the whole Society.

The early rules, already cited, had reference mainly to the mode of admission to membership, and the conduct of the periodical meetings of members. To these rules others were necessarily added at a later period, regulating the custody of the Society's property, and laying down conditions for the use of the same by Members. These scattered regulations do not appear to have been systematically codified until 1795, when, on the 1st of January, the following important Resolutions and " Laws " were ordered to be placed upon the Minutes :—

1st Jan., 1795. First—That the business of this Institution shall be conducted by a President, Vice-President, Treasurer, and Secretary, and a Committee of Eleven Members, under the control of the Society at large.

Second—That the object of this Society is the collection of an extensive Library, Philosophical Apparatus, and such productions of Nature and Art as tend to improve the mind and excite a spirit of general enquiry. This Society intends to collect such materials as will illustrate the antiquity, the natural, civil, commercial, and ecclesiastical history of this country. Provision has been made to render the Institution as permanent as the vicissitude of human affairs will permit, by making the Library and Museum a general and hereditary property. Donations of Books, Models of Machines, Specimens of Minerals, Animals, and Plants will be thankfully received ; and all communications relative to Arts, Natural Philosophy, and Literature, addressed to the Secretary for the time being, will be respectfully attended to.

Following these Resolutions are as many as forty-four Laws for the proper government of the Library, of which the following are among the most interesting :—

7th. That a British Shilling shall be paid by every Member of the Committee who shall be absent from any Meeting of the Society.

10th. That Ladies may be admitted Members of this Society, exempt from personal attendance, but in other respects amenable to the general rules. [1]

---

(1). Among ladies so admitted was Miss M'Cracken, after the death on the scaffold of her brother, Henry Joy M'Cracken, a member of Committee.

1st Jan., 1795.   11th. That no person shall be proposed to be balloted for as an honorary Member until he has received the approbation of the Committee.

13th. That the Admission Money be Two Guineas, and Subscription One British Shilling Monthly.

15th. That any Member lending a Book the property of the Society shall be subject to a fine of Ten Shillings.

17th. That Members who shall behave in a disorderly or refractory manner, or who refuse submission to the Laws, are to be expelled, on certain conditions stated.

23rd. That a Member may sell or bequeath his property in the Society; the transfer to be subject to the approval of the Committee.

31st. That no bound books shall be received from the bookseller that have not calfskin backs.

32nd. That no book shall be purchased bound in Leather which can be had in boards or stitched.

35th. That the Librarian shall attend all Meetings of the Society and its Committees under penalty of Double Fines.

41st. That the fine for keeping a book longer than the time limited shall be reduced to one penny per day; and the Librarian shall be paid the fines incurred on one book before he lends another.

44th. That no Article of the Philosophical Apparatus, nor such books of extraordinary value as may be selected by the Committee, shall be lent without their express consent; and, when so lent, Promissory Notes shall be given for their value, and also for such other Books as may exceed five guineas in price.

The original Rules fixed the number of the Committee of Management at Five Members. This number was subsequently increased to Nine, and again to Eleven; a quorum being Seven in the first instance, but afterwards Five.

The fines levied on Members for non-attendance at Meetings, and for the infringement of the Library Rules, appear to have been strictly enforced, and to have yielded a considerable addition to the income of the Society.[1]

The early Meetings of the Committee and Society were numerous, being generally held on Saturday evenings—at first weekly, afterwards fortnightly, and, later still, monthly. These meetings originally, and for several years, took place at taverns in the town— generally at " Ireland's," but occasionally also at " Brown's," " Drew's," and the " Donegal Arms." A Resolution passed in 1792 shows that this practice was not generally approved by the Members, who decided unanimously—

---

(1). Fines were on two occasions remitted, viz.:—To the Rev. Hugh O'Donnell, P.P., who resided in the country; and to Mr. Job Rider, who was " employed night and day in an important work closely "connected with some of the objects of this Institution." Until the completion of his *Steam Engine*, Mr. Rider was employed at the Foundry, Donegall Street; and on reference to the Catalogue, *Early Belfast Printed Books*, his name will be found there as an author (1801).

15th Aug., 1792. That it is the intention of the Society to remove their Meetings from a Public House immediately, and that this be the first business on the next Meeting of the Society.

But the wrath of the members appears to have been satisfied by this formal protest, as the matter was not referred to at the next or many subsequent meetings, and on April 6th, 1793, it was resolved at a General Meeting—

6th April, 1793. That the expences attending our Meeting at the "Donegall Arms" shall in future be paid by the Secretary out of the General Fund.

It was not till the Society removed to Ann Street, in 1794, that meetings began to be held in the Library.

The original regulation as to the admission of members by ballot, in which six black beans excluded, was subsequently modified so as to require the adverse votes of a quarter of the number present to veto an election; and to ensure the payment of the entrance money it was resolved, in 1792, to hold the proposer liable for this sum.

What was the amount of the original entrance fee, beyond the monthly subscription of a shilling British, is not recorded. Early in 1792, however, it was decided to raise the terms, and resolved—

7th Mar., 1792. That every new member proposed shall pay on his admission the sum of £2 5s 6d.

This rule does not appear to have interfered with the practice, not uncommon among new members, of giving books to the Library in lieu of entrance fee.

The rule requiring the quarterly election of the Committee remained in force till 1808, and therefore apparently worked well. Although we are led to suppose that a Secretary —James De Butts—was appointed on the formation of the Society in 1788, we find no record of the appointment of a President or Vice-President till 1792, when these officials were duly elected for a period of six months, a period which was shortly afterwards extended to a year. The offices of Secretary and Treasurer were at first held by the same person. In 1794 three Trustees were elected, in whose names the funds and property of the Society were to be duly vested. But no further action appears to have been taken in this matter.

An important change in the name of the Society was effected early in its history. In September, 1792, it was resolved—

1st Sept., 1792. That the Name of the Society shall be changed, and that the Committee shall consider a proper appellation for the Society.

This serious task does not appear to have occupied the Committee many days, and it was resolved on the 11th—

11th Sept., 1792. That the Society adopt the following appellation:—"The Belfast "Society for Promoting Knowledge."

The following Minutes show that in its early days the Society must have experienced considerable difficulty in providing funds sufficient for the proper carrying on of its work:—

16th April, 1792.   That this Society borrow one hundred pounds on their joint security for the purchase of books.

7th Sept., 1792.   That the Secretary shall be accountable for the fines incurred by the Members of the Society and of their Committees, or show cause.

6th Mar., 1794.   That the Society shall not proceed hereafter to Ballot for any person as a Member of this Society until the person proposing him pays down such sum as admission money as is then demanded.

19th Feb., 1795.   That the names of twenty or thirty of the principal Books added to the Library within the last Six Months be published in each of the Belfast Newspapers in such a manner that they shall not be charged as advertisements.

5th Oct., 1793.   That the Revd. Jas. Bryson and Doctor M'Donnell be requested to solicit Donations of Books from such persons as they think proper, and that the thanks of the Society shall hereafter be publickly returned for all Donations.

In September, 1792, a proposal was made by the " Belfast Book Society" for a union with the " Belfast Society for Promoting Knowledge." Committees were appointed on either side, and a conference and correspondence took place. But the business appears to have fallen through ; as also did a similar negotiation with the " Belfast Library" under the care of the Presbytery of Antrim.

The Society does not appear to have confined its proceedings on all occasions to the objects laid down in its Rules, and we find records of at least two important departures from its regular business. The first of these entered into the wider field of politics. The keen political excitement prevailing in Belfast during the early period of the Society's existence is sufficient explanation of the series of remarkable resolutions, passed on the 27th January, 1792, in favour of Catholic Emancipation, and extending the sympathy of the Members to the revolutionary movement at that time exercising so powerful an influence throughout Europe.—*(See Appendix A.)*

The second departure had far more relation to the objects of the Society, and indeed can scarcely be considered as foreign to its general aims. It was the consideration of a proposal by Dr. White, on the 3rd April, 1794, on the subject of Free Schools. The Doctor's long and closely reasoned plan is inserted on the Minutes, and will be found at Appendix B., and after hearing it, it was resolved—

3rd April, 1794.   That a Committee of ten be chosen for the purpose of considering of the best mode of carrying the scheme into effect, and calling on the inhabitants of this town individually for Subscriptions for the establishment of a Free School, and that as soon as they have executed that business, the Committee should be requested to call a Meeting of the Subscribers for the purpose of enacting laws for the Government of the Institution.

This resolution was afterwards confirmed, and a Committee duly appointed to carry out the undertaking ; but there is no further allusion to the subject on the Minutes.

III.

The Formation of the Library and Museum.

IT is hardly necessary to state that no entries in the old Minute Books of the Belfast Reading Society are more interesting than those which relate to the formation of the nucleus of the fine Library which is at present on the shelves of the Linen Hall.

The founders of the Society were evidently much in earnest as to their responsibilities in this direction, and went about their work with considerable judgment and care. At the outset of their operations, however, the scheme narrowly escaped shipwreck in consequence of the following extraordinary regulation, passed unanimously at a General Meeting of the Society (on the recommendation of the Committee), on March 7th, 1792 :—

7th Mar., 1792. That every future member of their Committee shall upon his admission sign a declaration that while he is in office he will not consent to the choice or purchase of any Book which is not in the English Language, or any common Novel or farce, or other book of trivial amusement.

This regulation was in operation for several months, and it was not till the 11th September, in the same year. at the same meeting at which the name of the Society was changed, that the following relaxation of the rule was adopted :—

11th Sept., 1792. That the Rule preventing the purchase of Antient and Foreign Literature be rescinded.

That not more than one-fifth of the Annual Subscription shall be applied to the purchase of Ancient and Foreign Literature.

It would appear that the restriction respecting "Novels, farces, and books of trivial amusement" still remained in force ; and it is due to the Committee of that day to add that they showed no disposition to transgress in that direction.

A further initial difficulty was the want of funds. In April, 1792, it was decided to borrow £100, on the joint security of the members, for the purchase of books. It would seem, however, that the entrance fees, subscriptions, and fines in a short time placed the Society in a position, with the exercise of much caution and economy, to pay its own way without assistance from without.

The first Minute on the records relating to the purchase of books occurs on November 5th, 1791, when it was resolved—

5th Nov., 1791. That the Secretary shall purchase Robertson's History of Scotland, Kame's Essays and Sketches of the History of Man, the most approved History of Ireland, and inform himself, previous to the next meeting of the Committee, of the price of Buffon's Natural History, with coloured and uncoloured plates.

One of these wants was supplied two meetings later by Mr. Robert Cary, who presented a copy of Dr. Curry's History of Ireland, for which he received the thanks of the Society ; and at the first meeting, in 1792, the Secretary was instructed to procure—

2nd Jan., 1792.

        Buffon's Natural History.
        Robertson's Disquisitions Concerning India.
        Encyclopædia Britannica.
        Kello Sermons.
        Analytical Reviews.
        Anacharsis' Travels.
        Travels through Greece.
        Mitford's History of Greece.

    In March the same year the following important purchases were ordered :—

3rd Mar., 1792.   Dr. Gillies's History of Greece.
        Transactions of the Royal Society of London.
        Transactions of the Royal Irish Academy.
        Transactions of the Bath and Manchester Societies.
        Dodsley's Annual Register, commencing with the year 1788.

    With regard to the Transactions, an instruction was added to the agent " to go as far " back in each series as can be gotten complete."   At the meeting after this the resolution excluding " Foreign and ancient literature and books of trivial amusement" was passed, and the Society proceeded to purchase —

10th Mar., 1792.   Transactions of the Edinburgh Philosophical Society.
        Lavater's Aphorisms.
        Dr. Burney's History of Music.

    It would be impossible in the space at our disposal to give anything like a catalogue of the early purchases of the Society, but we may note the following works of special value or interest :—

14th April, 1792.   Johnson's Lives of the Poets.
        Pope's Works, the best edition.
        Hume and Smollett's History of England.

5th July, 1792.   Observations on the Volcanoes of the Two Sicilies, with coloured plates.
        Collection of Etruscan, Greek, and Roman Antiquities, 2 vols.

22nd Aug., 1792.   An Atlas.
        Monasticon Hibernicum.
        Priestley's History of Electricity.
        Asiatic Researches.

22nd Sept., 1792.   Boswell's Life of Johnson.
        Cook's Voyages and Life, to be compleat with his Voyages now in
             the Library.
        Evelyn's Sylva.
        Philosophical Transactions of the Society of Philadelphia.
        Transactions of the Royal Society of Edinburgh.
        Monro's Treatise upon Fishes.

11th Oct., 1792.   Memoir of the French Academy of Arts.

Transactions of the Imperial Academy of St. Petersburg.

Transactions of the Society in London for encouraging Arts, Manufactures, and Commerce.

Biographia Britannica.

Sir Joshua Reynolds' Lectures to the Academicians.

Walpole's Lives of the Painters.

The above selection will give an idea of the comprehensive and wise spirit with which the first members laid the foundation of the Library. It may be mentioned here that the particular object for which the £100, already referred to, was borrowed, is explained in the following Minute, which is interesting as marking the value at that time set upon the work to which it refers :—

18th April, 1792.   Resolved—That the Society purchase the Philosophical Transactions of the Royal Society of London complete, to be sold at Daly's Auction, 1st May, and such other scarce Works, and under such restrictions, as the Committee may deem necessary. The sum to be laid out not to exceed One Hundred Pounds.

That this important order was duly and satisfactorily executed is evident from the following Resolution of June 2nd :—

2nd June, 1792.   That the Secretary write a letter of thanks to Mr. Robert Callwell for his care and attention in the purchase of the Philosophical Transactions, and for his generous and unsolicited offer of credit to the Society.

The acquisitions of the Library by no means consisted only of books purchased. The gifts made by members were numerous, and deserve grateful record in this short History. A catalogue of such donations appears at one time to have existed, but is unfortunately not now to be found. But as these gifts were recorded, from time to time, upon the Minutes, it will be both interesting and proper here to give a list of such during the first ten years of the Society's existence : —

1788-98.	*Benefactor.*		*Gift.*
	Mr. R. Cary ...	...	Curry's History of Ireland.
	Mr. Wm. M'Cleery ...	...	Physical and Literary Essays.
	Mr. Jas. Kirker ...	...	The Works of Lord Chesterfield.
	Mr. R. Grueber ...	...	Elegant Extracts.
	Dr. M'Donnell ...	...	Mickle's Translation of the Lusiad.
	Do. ...	...	Donaldson's Military Tactics.
	Do. ...	...	Sacheverall's Tryal.
	Do. ...	...	Kirwan on Acids and Salts.
	Mr. Geo. B. Madden	...	Dacier's Horace, in Latin.
	Do. ...	...	Amsterdam in 1735. Very elegant.
	Do. ...	...	Hoole's Trans. of Tasso's Jerusalem. Elegant.

1788-98.	*Benefactor.*	*Gift.*
Mr. Wm. Thos. Atkinson	...	Clayton's Vindication of the New Testament. 3 vols.
Do.	...	Cat. of Books Published in London, 1700-1779.
Mr. John Haslett	...	Chaucer's Works.
Mr. M. Spottiswood	...	Cowley's Works.
Mr. R. M'Cormick	...	Keil's Introduction to Nat. Philosophy.
Do.	...	His. of Great Britain. By John Speed.
Mr. John Templeton	...	Cunn's Euclid.
Mr. Rainey Maxwell	...	Journals of the House of Commons.
Do.	...	Index to Do.—Last xi. vols.—1763.
Do.	...	The British Constitution.
Mr. Wm. Sampson	...	Law Catalogue. Dublin, 1790.
Do.	...	Cat. of Pictures, &c., in the Shakespeare Gallery.
Do.	...	Piso's Collection—East and West Indies.
Do.	...	Christie's Letters on the French Revolution.
Mr. Roger Mulholland	...	Cæsar's Commentaries Trans. Duncan.
Do.	...	Vitruvius Britannicus. 3 vols.
Dr. B. Fuller	...	Universal History. 20 vols.
Do.	...	Bonham's Chemistry.
Miss Legg, Bridge Street	...	Grotius. 3 vols. 8vo.
Mr. Jas. Scott	...	Cohausen's Experiments, &c.
Do.	...	Dr. Black's MS. Lectures on Chemistry.
Mr. Robt. Callwell	...	Burnet's History of his own Time. 6 vols.
Do.	...	Beatson's Political Index to His. Britain and Ireland.
Do.	...	Marsden's Sumatra.
Do.	...	Langhorne on Ancient Italian Republic.
Do.	...	Whitaker's Review of Gibbon.
Alderman Boydell	...	100 Prints. Engraved and Drawn by Himself.
Mr. Wm. Osborne	...	On Government. By Algernon Sidney.
Mr. Charles Lynd	...	A Bible in the Irish Language.
Miss Eliza Wallace	...	Robison's Proofs of a Conspiracy Against all the Religions and Governments of Europe.
Royal Irish Academy	...	Transactions R.I.A.
Mr. Thompson	...	Tytler's Historical Register.

Another means by which the Library was occasionally recruited arose from the regulation which was in operation from an early date, that new Members might commute their Entrance Fee by a gift of books to the Library of the same value. We subjoin a list of books thus received from Mr. Andrew Beard in 1793, which is of special interest, as indicating what in those days was considered fair value for Two Guineas sterling.

Books offered by Mr. Beard in lieu of Admission Money (Two Guineas).

2nd May, 1793. A French Translation of Seneca. By Charloit.

A Treatise of Geography, from the French. By E. Grimstone.

Translation of Polanos' His. Council of Trent.

Acts passed from II. to XI. Year of Queen Anne.

Atkinson's Epitome of Navigation.

Historical Essays. By Jerome Alley.

Traité de l'Âmes des Bêtes.

The Dignity and Honor of the Clergy represented. By John Groome.

Remarks on the Characters of the English and French Ladies. By John Andrews, LL.D.

Helsham's Lectures.

A Table of Public Statutes from V. to XI. of King George.

An Abridgement of all the Statutes from the End of Queen Anne to the VI. of George.

An Abridgement of all the Statutes of William and Mary and of William III. and Anne.

Complete Land Steward's Assistant. By Giles Jacob.

A similar transaction is noted on February 20, 1793, when we find that Mr. Samuel Robinson offered two octavo volumes (a portion of a set) of Curtis's Botanical Magazine in lieu of entrance money. The offer was accepted, and it was resolved that the Society should subscribe for the remainder of the set and its continuation.

The early members appear to have kept well in view the special objects for which their Society was founded. Besides the scientific collection, to which reference will be made shortly, they exerted themselves to make the Library thoroughly representative of all branches of Literature and Fine Art. Their attention was directed in 1792 to the Art publications of the famous Alderman Boydell, of London ; and on Oct. 27 it was resolved—

27th Oct., 1792. That the Secretary be requested to correspond with Alderman Boydell with the view of ascertaining the path the Society should pursue in making Collections of Books relative to the Fine Arts; and the Committee recommends to the Society that they shall make a Collection of Specimens in the Fine Arts, to commence with the Purchase of Wedgwood's impressions of Antient Medals.

The Alderman's reply to this communication was the gift of a book containing 100 prints, engraved and drawn by himself, for which he was thanked by the Society, and at once elected an Honorary Member.

Early in 1793 a suggestion was made that the Society should make a special effort to secure various books printed in the Irish Language ; and the following Resolution was passed accordingly :—

2nd Mar., 1793.   That Mr. Callwell be requested to write, in the name of the Society, to such gentlemen as he knows to be possessed of Books or MSS. in the Irish Language, intimating the desire of the Society to procure such, and expressing their grateful thanks for all such donations ; and that the Standing Committee be empowered to expend a sum not exceeding Ten Guineas in purchasing such Books and MSS.

This appeal may have been suggested by the gift, at the same meeting, of a Bible in the Irish Language, by Mr. Charles Lynd, of Coleraine. This acquisition appears to have been highly prized, as Mr. Lynd was almost immediately afterwards elected an Honorary Member. It is to be regretted that Mr. Callwell's appeal does not appear to have resulted at the time in any further donations of Irish books.

The Minutes, however, make it evident that everything associated with the ancient inhabitants of Ireland, which was worthy to be admired, was highly prized by the Members, who fully realized the responsibility of the Society in the matter. In proof of this, the following Minutes are of peculiar interest :—

7th Mar., 1793.   It having been reported to the Committee that a Collection of old Irish Music, superior to any hitherto published, was made at the late Meeting of the Irish Harpers, at Belfast,

Resolved—That it be recommended to the Society to take said work under its patronage ; to publish it in London under the name of the Society, with a prefatory Discourse, allowing the Profits derived therefrom to the person who took down the Notes ; and that a letter be written and signed by the Chairman to Mr. Edward Bunting, informing him of the Society's intention.

This offer was accepted by Mr. Bunting, and the work undertaken ; and at the Meeting in April, 1794, it was unanimously resolved—

3rd April, 1794.   That £50 be transmitted to Mr. R. Jamieson, of London, to be expended in the Printing of the Irish Music collected by Mr. Bunting, according to the engagements formerly made by the Society.

The Mr. Jamieson here referred to acted as London agent to the Society, having been appointed to that post in Feb., 1793, for the purpose of transacting business and effecting purchases in the metropolis.

The last we hear of the business of the Irish Music is in 1798, when Mr. Callwell reported—

18th Jan., 1798.   That he has received from Mr. Edward Bunting £34 : 3 : 4, a part of the money which the Society advanced to Mr. Bunting for the purpose of forwarding the Irish Music.[1]

The early Committee appear to have exercised a careful oversight of the Books committed to their care. In March, 1793, a set of rules, for the guidance of the Librarian, was drawn up for adoption by the Society, which, as they subsequently became part of the Laws of the Society, it will be interesting to summarise here :—

16th Mar., 1793.   1. The Librarian, or his Deputy, to attend daily, from 11 to 2.

2. The Catalogue to be alphabetical, and to give particulars as to Author, Title, Edition, Case and Shelf No., price, No. of vols., and size.

3. Books only to be delivered on personal application or signed order of Member. No Member to have out more than one vol. at a time.

4. Philosophical Apparatus and Books of great value only to be lent out with the Committee's consent, the borrower to give a promissory note for the full value of same.

5. Strict account of books lent, and the condition in which they are returned, to be kept, and forfeitures levied for injuries done.

6. The Librarian responsible for all the property of the Society under his care, and for the enforcement of the rules of the Library.

7. Penalty for not returning books punctually must be enforced. The Librarian may renew a loan; and Members residing more than two miles from Belfast may have 6 days' grace allowed.

8. The Librarian must attend all meetings of the Society and Committee under penalty of double fines.

The two following Minutes show that Rule 4 was strictly acted upon :—

27th Nov., 1794.   That Mr. Job Rider have the loan of the Philosophical Transactions for 1777, on giving the Librarian a Promissory Note for £100, to be given up on return of the Book.

That Mr. Ferris have the loan of the 1st vol. of the Biographia Britannica, on giving a Promissory Note for £9, to be given up on return of the Book.

The term for which books might be borrowed had been fixed in Sept., 1792, viz. :— For an 8vo volume, 14 days; for a 4to volume, 30 days; and for a Folio volume, 2 calendar months.

The Minutes bear ample testimony to the jealous care of the Committees for the Society's property. A yearly revision took place, and books which were found wanting were advertised for in the papers. The Librarian was frequently called upon to report

---

(1). Mr. Benn, in the continuation of his *History of Belfast* (London, 1880, 8vo), p. 210, gives an interesting sketch of the life and career of this Irish musical enthusiast, supplied to him by our townsman, Mr. C. H. Brett, and states that Mr. Bunting's first volume—probably the one here referred to—was published in 1796, though not, apparently, in the name of the Society. From this collection Moore derived a large number of the most beautiful of his "Irish Melodies."

overdue volumes ; and Inspectors were appointed to check over the books with the Librarian's list ; also to examine all new purchases, bindings, and estimates. Occasional Minutes are found ordering the binding of particular books ; but in April, 1793, a general regulation directed the Librarian

20th April, 1793.   To have all the Books in the Library half-bound, with corners and lettered, as speedily as may be consistent with the convenience of members.

About the same time, the trouble and delay connected with the procuring of books from London and Dublin, as well as a desire to encourage the industry of the town, suggested the expediency of the following resolution :—

7th Mar., 1793.   That such books as may be ordered by the Committee shall be purchased in Belfast, if possible ; and that such as cannot be so procured shall be ordered through the Correspondents of the Belfast Booksellers.

The caution of the Committee with regard to money matters has already been alluded to. We come upon occasional Minutes ordering that, in view of the present condition of the Funds, the "proposal book" shall be shut up, and all purchases suspended. As a rule, however, the Committee were in a position to order the purchase of books at most of their meetings ; and occasionally the Secretary's financial report shows a good balance in hand.

It is unfortunate that the old financial statements of the Society have not been preserved ; so that the Minute book affords our only means of judging of the amount of their income and expenditure. We may, however, quote one of these statements, made on April 4th, 1793, as indicative of the funds with which the Society at that period had to deal.

4th April, 1793.   The Secretary's report of the State of the Funds this day is—

	£	s.	d.
Clear cash in hand	£67	0	8
Admission money due	111	9	6
Subscription do.	35	8	6
	£213	18	8
Probable amt. of Books ordered ...	100	0	0
Balance in favour of the Society ...	£113	18	8

The first notice of a Catalogue on the Minutes is on Mar. 28th, 1793, when the Rev. Jas. Bryson and Mr. John Templeton were requested to prepare one. This was done, and at the next meeting following it was resolved—

4th April, 1793.   That it be printed under their Superintendence, with an addition, in Italics, of the Books now ordered ; and, as a preface to it, the 1st, 3rd, 4th, 5th, 6th, and 7th Rules of regulations for the Librarian (see proceedings of the Committee, 16th March), and the 10th, 11th, and 15th Rules of the printed Regulations, with such alterations as may seem necessary.

It is unfortunate that no copy of this first Catalogue of the Library can be found. It was printed during the summer of the year, and at the October meeting it was resolved—

5th Oct., 1793. That the Secretary be requested to transmit to each member who has not yet paid his admission money a Copy of the Laws, a Catalogue of the Books, and a request that he will, as soon as possible, pay his admission.

A second Catalogue was put in hand in November, 1794, of which 400 copies were ordered to be printed, each member to receive one copy gratis. A special Catalogue of the Scientific Books in the Library was also undertaken, under the superintendence of five of the members.

These two Catalogues are also unfortunately missing, although it is recorded that the second general Catalogue was complete in April, 1795.

The Society do not for a moment appear to have lost sight of that important branch of their duties which consisted in providing a collection of scientific and natural history objects, with a view to form the beginning of a Museum for the use of its members.

As early as September, 1792, we find this Minute :—

11th Sept., 1792. That the Society shall take some immediate steps towards the purchase of a compleat Philosophical Apparatus, and that a Correspondence be commenced with Sir William Jones.

Of this correspondence and its results we have no formal record, but the Committee proceeded at once to secure copies of scientific works, aiming specially to form a collection of the transactions of the learned societies. The first purchase of a scientific instrument is noted in March, 1793, when an air-pump, after being carefully inspected and reported upon by Mr. Rider, was ordered to be purchased at the price of four guineas.[1]

In the same month Mr. John Templeton, an eminent local botanist, who had also served as Secretary to the Society, was requested

2nd Mar., 1793. To superintend the Botanical part of the Institution, and to use every effort in procuring a Hortus Siccus for the Museum, and in this department to attend the Committees in future.

At a later meeting Dr. M'Donnell and Mr. Templeton were appointed a sub-committee "for the purpose of ordering a portfolio for the preservation of plants;" also a cabinet fit to contain fossils and curiosities ; and Mr. Templeton was further asked to take charge of Dickson's collection of dried plants "until he can get them properly "secured in their places."

These purchases were followed up by the acquisition of two barometers, two thermometers, and a rain gauge; also a hygrometer and eudiometer; and later on a Wedgwood's pyrometer.[2]

A great impetus was given to the Museum of the Society by the gift, in 1796, of a valuable box of fossils from Dr. Forster, of Hamburg. Dr. Forster was immediately made

---

(1). Very shortly after its purchase we find a note that the air-pump had to be sent back to Mr. Rider for repair.

(2). Dr. Malcolm, in his *History of the General Hospital, Belfast*, 1851 (p. 19) speaks of the Society as "chiefly devoted to the accumulation of a library and the record of atmospheric phenomena." "A "register for the weather" was kept by the Librarian.

an Honorary Member; and a suitable cabinet was ordered for the reception of the gift.[1]
Subsequently the Secretary was "requested to obtain a specimen of Wicklow gold to send
" to Mr. Forster, agreeable to his request."

The following Minute will show the importance attached by members to the orderly
and careful custody of the collections under their care :—

5th May, 1796.   That at the general Meeting of the Society, usually held in May
                        every Year, Three Members shall be chosen by Ballot as Inspectors, whose
                        duty it shall be to examine and report as to the state of the stock of the
                        Association ; whether the Books are in good condition, and whether the
                        stock as purchased or possessed by the Society is entire, and to remark
                        whether any Books are lost or unaccounted for ; the state of the Philo-
                        sophical Instruments, of Paintings, Prints, and dry Vegetable and Animal
                        Preparations, every Mineral, Fossil, and other object of Natural History,
                        as well as every other property appertaining to the Society ; and that the
                        said Inspectors do give in under their hands at every general Meeting of
                        the Society, in the months of May and November respectively, their
                        written report on these subjects for the examination of the Society.

The first three inspectors under this regulation were Drs. Bruce, White, and
Stephenson. Their report does not appear on the Minutes.

IV.

The Early Office-Bearers of the Society.

IN our opening note a list is found of the Members of the Belfast Reading Society
who attached their names to the original copy of the rules drawn up May 13th, 1788.
Of these, eighteen are distinguished as Founders of the Society.

Any reader conversant with the history of Belfast during the agitated period
covered by the first few years of the Society's existence cannot fail to have observed
that the men who took the most active part in conducting its affairs were also among
the most prominent citizens of the town, and active participators in the political and
social movements of the day. It may be interesting, in closing this first portion of
our work, to recall a few of these names, adding such personal notes as are afforded by
the best known histories of the town.

Presidents.—The Society, as has been noticed, did not proceed to the election of
a PRESIDENT till the meeting of Oct. 6th, 1792, when Dr. ALEX. HALIDAY (who, on the
previous day, had been admitted a member) was unanimously elected. His letter
accepting the office is recorded on the Minutes, under date 11th Oct. :—

(1). This cabinet (which cost twelve guineas) was the subject of several Minutes at the time of the removal
of the Library and Museum to Donegall Street. On the 3rd April, 1800, it was reported that "it could
" not be accommodated in the present apartments of the Society." It appears to have been kept in the
Academy Library for some time, its key being committed to the custody of the President of the Society.
In 1801, another effort was made to get it into the Society's premises, which succeeded, the cost of the
removal being noted 9s 9d. It is now in the Museum, College Square.

11th Oct., 1792. SIR,—I have this instant received your notification of my being appointed President of "The Belfast Society for Promoting Knowledge;" and I beg you may take the first opportunity of expressing my high sense of the Honour they have done me—an Honour which I very cheerfully embrace. To improve and diffuse Knowledge, is to improve man, and extend those inestimable blessings, Virtue, Order, and Liberty. I sincerely hope and trust this Laudable Institution will be productive of all the good the Members have in view. My feeble co-operation shall not be wanting. I beg, Sir, that you will assure the other Gentlemen whose names appear at the foot of your letter, of my particular respects.—I am, Sir, with great regard, your faithfull and obliged servant, A. HALIDAY.

Mr. ROBERT M'CORMICK,
    Secretary of the Society for Promoting Knowledge.
      10th Oct., 1792.

Dr. Alexander Haliday does not appear to have attended many meetings either of the Committee or Society; but, on account of his popularity and eminence, he was continued in office till 1798.

Of Dr. Haliday, Doctor Malcolm says—"His popularity as a Physician extended "through the entire province of Ulster; and he was no less distinguished for "his elegant accomplishments, his patriotic spirit, and his moral worth."[1] Benn numbers him among the literary persons in Belfast in the eighteenth century; and mentions that he was the author of a tragedy and many poetical pieces.

Dr. Haliday's part in the political excitement of the town was of a moderating character; and on the occasion of the invasion of Belfast by the "Hearts of Steel," he acted as mediator between the insurgents and the authorities, surrendering himself as a hostage to the former as an earnest of his good faith. To his efforts was largely due the pacification of this dangerous outbreak.

His name appears in connection with the leading philanthropic and social movements of the day. He died, much regretted, in 1802, having bequeathed a very valuable and extensive collection of books to the Library.

As a testimony to his reputation for learning and benevolence, may be quoted an extract from Arthur Young's *Tour Through Ireland*, 1779, where he says—"Went to "Castle Hill, Mr. Townley Blackwood's. In the evening, at Belfast, at dinner at Mr. "Blackwood's, a Dr. Haliday was mentioned as a gentleman of general knowledge, and, "at the same time, of a liberal disposition. I determined to make known to this Dr. "Haliday my wants, and beg his assistance in gratifying them."

His nephew, Dr. WILLIAM HALIDAY, was admitted a member in 1800, and took an active part in the business of the Society afterwards.

Dr. WM. BRUCE, who succeeded Dr. Haliday as President, had already served the Society four years as Vice-President. He was Minister of the First Presbyterian Church

---

[1]. *General Hospital*, p. 53.—In quoting this authority, it may not be considered out of place to mention that several of the beautiful illustrations which adorn Dr. Malcolm's book are taken from copperplates engraved by the late John Thomson, of Castle Street. This art, which locally had reached to a high degree of excellence, has been sadly interfered with by the Photographer.

(Unitarian), Belfast, and Principal of the Belfast Academy, an Institution founded by Dr. Crombie, in 1786, as a seminary for the education of the better classes of citizens. Under Dr. Bruce, who had been a distinguished scholar of Trinity College, Dublin, the school attained its greatest celebrity, and attracted scholars from all parts of Ireland. His Presidency extended from 1798 till 1817, but he remained afterwards for many years associated with the Society. He died in 1841, aged 84. His family, it is said, claim descent from the Royal family of Bruce of Scotland. The accompanying Portrait of this estimable gentleman is taken from a Painting in oil at the Library, presented to the Society by Mr. William B. Joy.

Vice-Presidents.—The first VICE-PRESIDENT of the Society was Mr. ROBERT BRADSHAW, one of the original partners in the Commercial Bank, Belfast, who was appointed on November 3rd, 1792. His name appears for some years as an active member of Committees.

In 1794 he was succeeded by Dr. BRUCE, on whose appointment to the Presidency, in 1798, the Rev. PATRICK VANCE was elected Vice-President. Mr. Vance, a man who was held in universal respect, was minister of the Second Presbyterian Church of Belfast, where he had succeeded the Rev. James Bryson in 1791. His term of office was a short one, as he died in 1800.

His successor, Mr. JOHN HOLMES, an eminent banker and member of an old Belfast family, had already served the Society as Treasurer. He only acted as Vice-President for a short time, and was succeeded in 1801 by his kinsman, Mr. ROBERT HOLMES, a merchant. Mr. John Holmes died in 1825, aged 80.

In 1802, Mr. Robert Holmes was succeeded in the Vice-Presidency by Dr. S. M. STEPHENSON, one of the foremost medical practitioners in Belfast, whose name was well known in connection with the medical and philanthropic institutions of the town in his day. He continued to take a very active part in the business of the Society for many years. He died in 1833. Previous to his settlement in Belfast as a physician, he had been the Presbyterian minister of Greyabbey, County Down.

Secretaries.—The first SECRETARY of the Society was Mr. JAMES DE BUTTS, who was one of the original founders in 1788. For some years the offices of Secretary and Treasurer appear to have been combined. Mr. De Butts retained office till 1792, when he went abroad, and was succeeded by Mr. ROBERT M'CORMICK, who, however, only remained in office nine months. He was succeeded by Mr. WILLIAM CLARKE,[1] who acted as Secretary only, Mr. John Holmes taking the duties of Treasurer. Mr. Clarke's period of office was very brief, since, before the beginning of the next year (1794), Mr. GEO. B. MADDEN's name is found as Secretary. Mr. Madden gave in his resignation in January of the same year; and in the following August Mr. JOHN TEMPLETON,[2] the celebrated naturalist and

(1). He was usually known as Mr. Clarke, "the magistrate," and was father to the late John Clarke, Esq., J.P., Chairman for many years of the Harbour Commissioners, and Mayor of Belfast, 1871-2.
(2). Mr. Templeton had taken charge of the botanical collections of the Society from the beginning. He enjoyed a European reputation, and for the last thirty years of his life was actively employed in forming collections for a Natural History of Ireland. He was awarded a prize by the Royal Dublin Society, and

The REV. WILLIAM BRUCE, D.D.,
PRESIDENT, 1798-1817.

botanist, who since January had been discharging the duties of Secretary without appointment, also retired, whereupon Mr. ROBERT SIMMS[1] was chosen for one year. In February, 1796, the Secretary appointed was Mr. GILBERT M'ILVEEN, jun., who acted till August, 1797, when, owing to his absence abroad, his post was taken by Mr. JAMES MUNFOAD, an appointment which evidently gave satisfaction, as it was renewed for many years in succession.

It will thus be seen that between 1792 and 1797 the post of Secretary changed hands no less than seven times. The work was undoubtedly onerous and responsible, and the Minutes bear ample testimony to the fact that, during their brief terms of office, most of the Secretaries devoted considerable time and energy to the business of the Society.

Two of the above-named Secretaries—Mr. Robert Simms and Mr. Gilbert M'Ilveen—were among the founders of the famous *Northern Star* newspaper in 1792, and were intimately connected with the revolutionary movement which agitated the town during the few years which followed. The latter was one of the early directors of the first Belfast Bank, known as the Discount Office.

Librarians.—During the period before 1800 three Librarians held office under the Society. The first was Mr. ROBERT CARY, one of the original founders, who was appointed at the meeting of May 5th, 1792, at which it was resolved—

5th May, 1792. That a Librarian be appointed to take care of and deliver the books to the members of the Society.

The books, as has been stated, were transferred in the following March to Mr. Cary's house, and kept there until February, 1794, when, he having retired, Mr. Thomas Russell was appointed Librarian. The Library during his time was removed to the house in Ann Street.

Mr. THOMAS RUSSELL was a remarkable man, who played a memorable part in the politics of Belfast in his day. In 1791 he visited Belfast as an ensign of a regiment of foot. In the same year, quitting the service, he revisited the town with his intimate friend Theobald Wolf Tone, and became a contributor to the *Northern Star*, and a founder of the Society of United Irishmen. In the troubles which ensued he shared the prosecution and ultimately the fate of some of his friends, and was executed in the year 1803. Benn states of Russell that, " for his literary taste, general deportment, and unbounded love of " liberty, he became a great favourite. So much regard was felt for him that, when it was " feared he might entangle himself beyond recovery in dangerous schemes, every effort " was made to detach him from the United Irishmen."[2]

---

afterwards a medal by the Belfast Natural History and Philosophical Society, for the discovery of the " Rosa Hibernica," which he found, A.D. 1795, on the left of the old road going to Holywood. This rose is represented on the seal of the Holywood Town Commissioners in conjunction with a "sphere"—the latter being taken from a Treatise by Joannes de Sacro Bosco, entitled *De Sphæra Mundi*.

(1). Grandfather to Mr. Felix B. Simms, Chamberlain to the Committee of the Proprietors of the Linen Hall.

(2). *History of Belfast*, p. 644.—In Dr. R. R. Madden's account of Samuel Neilson, Editor of the *Northern Star*, it is recorded that, on the occasion of the arrest of the proprietors in 1796, Neilson " went into the Public Library belonging to the Society for Promoting Knowledge, where Mr. Pollock " and Lord Downshire were in pursuit of something, and gave himself into custody."

Mr. Russell devoted much time and attention to the affairs of the Society, particularly in their difficult search for premises, the negotiations for which he himself conducted.

On the abrupt termination of Mr. Russell's duties at the Library in 1796, Mr. JOHN M'COUGHTRY[1] offered his services to the Society "for that duty until Mr. Russell's return," and was subsequently formally installed as his successor. He held office till 1802, when Mr. JAMES SLOAN, immediately after the removal of the Library to the Linen Hall, was appointed, and continued to act as Librarian for several years.

During the period under consideration, seven HONORARY MEMBERS were admitted, in the following order :—

1791 Rev. Jas. Bryson	1792 R. Grueber	1793 Chas. Lynd
1792 John M'Coughtry	1792 Alderman Boydell	1794 Job Rider

and 1796 Dr. Forster

With regard to the COMMITTEES OF MANAGEMENT, a complete list will be found in the Appendix. We may, however, mention a few of the principal names on the list in the early years.

The first Committee on the Minutes (Nov. 1st, 1791) consisted of five members, viz.:—

Robert M'Cormick	Robt. Cary
James M'Cormick	John Rabb

Maurice Spottiswood

Of these, John Rabb became notorious as the printer of the famous *Northern Star*, for which he was tried and found guilty, and his entire plant seized and destroyed.

In April, 1792, the Committee was increased to nine. Among the early members was the Rev. JAS. BRYSON (Honorary). He had been the third minister in succession of the Second Presbyterian Church, and was the first minister of the Donegall Street Presbyterian Church. He was also author of a volume of Sermons and of several Discourses—(see Catalogue, *Early Belfast Printed Books*, 1787).[2]

Dr. JAMES M'DONNELL was one of the original Founders of the Society, and an active Member of the Committee in its early days. He was an eminent local doctor and scientist, and was prominently connected with the founding of the Medical Charities of the town, including the General Hospital, of which he was the first Physician. An interesting account of him is given in Benn's continuation of the *History of Belfast*, vol. ii., page 157. In recognition of the respect and esteem in which he was held by the community, and of the eminent services which he rendered in assisting to lay the foundation of the Belfast Natural History and Philosophical Society, a marble bust of him was placed in the Museum, from which the accompanying representation is taken.

At a subsequent meeting the number of the Committee was increased to eleven; and among the new members was Mr. ROBERT CALLWELL, a banker, who, perhaps, did more for the Library at the time than anyone else. He not only made advances of money when necessary, but, at a later date, printed one of the appendices to the catalogue

---

(1). Said to be of Wood's and Macoughtry's School, North Street. (See advt. *Dr. Lowth's Grammar*, 1765).

(2). He was great grandfather of Mr. Samuel Bryson, of Holywood.

JAMES McDONNELL, Esq., M.D.,
A FOUNDER AND ACTIVE MEMBER OF COMMITTEE, 1788-1817.

at his own cost. He also made many valuable gifts of books, and took an active and useful part in the deliberations of the Committee. Among the other more prominent members who built up the Library may be mentioned the following :—

Rev. JOHN CLARKE, Curate to the Rev. Wm. Bristow, Vicar of Belfast, and Sovereign, for many years, of the town : Mr. Clarke was most active in the establishment of a Dispensary for the poor. COUNSELLOR SAMPSON, famous for his defence of the proprietors of the *Northern Star* at their two trials; JAMES HYNDMAN, grandfather to Hugh Hyndman, LL.D., solicitor: he was a Notary Public, and for some time acted as Town Clerk ; DAVID BIGGER, a merchant in High Street, and regular attendant at Committees till 1813, whose son, Mr. Joseph Bigger, of Ardrie, and two grandsons, Edward Coey Bigger, M.D., and Francis Joseph Bigger, solicitor, are still with us ; RAINEY MAXWELL, a retired shipowner and merchant, residing at Greenville ; THOMAS M'DONNELL (who afterwards served as Secretary), father of the well-known Counsellor of that name, residing at Eglinton ; JOHN HOLMES HOUSTON, ancestor of Blakiston Houston, V.L., Co. Down ; THOS. BATESON, grandfather of Lord Deramore ; THOS. B. ISAAC, of Holywood House ; JOHN TURNLEY, of Rockport, and his brother ALEXANDER ; JOHN GREGG, Merchant ; HENRY J. TOMBE; JAMES FERGUSON, of Newforge Bleach Works ; WM. SINCLAIRE, of the Falls and other Bleachgreens; JOHN S. FERGUSON, Linen Merchant, also Bleacher and Paper Manufacturer; WILLIAM TENNENT, Merchant and Banker, father-in-law to Sir James Emerson Tennent, Bart. ; NICHOLAS GRIMSHAW, who first introduced Calico Printing into the neighbourhood ; ROBERT GETTY, father of the late Edmund Getty, a well known Antiquarian ; WADDELL CUNNINGHAM, a conspicuous character, and frequently Chairman at Public Meetings, which were very common in those days : he was also Captain of the 4th Company of the Belfast Yeomanry Infantry ; HENRY JOY and two of his brothers, grandsons of Francis Joy, the founder of the *Belfast News-Letter.* Henry Joy is described as one of the very few men really acquainted with the history of Belfast. He was the author of a valuable work on the subject, published in 1817 by Geo. Berwick, and, in conjunction with Dr. Bruce, of a series of papers known as *Belfast Politicks.* He died in 1835. The name of one of the founders of the Library, ROGER MULHOLLAND, must not be omitted. He was in his time an eminent builder and surveyor, and to him—under the direction of Mr. Talbot, agent to Lord Donegal—the town is very much indebted for its wide streets, as it was he who was employed to lay out in streets and squares that part of the town in the neighbourhood of the Linen Hall. He was grandfather to the late Dr. Cunningham Mulholland, of this town.

Not to continue these references much further, it may be stated that the list of Members and Committees shows that a large proportion of the most active members of the Society were also the leading men in and around Belfast—the men, in fact, who laid the foundation of its present proud position as a mercantile and manufacturing centre, and to whom we are largely indebted for the number and excellence of our Schools, Hospitals, and Charitable Institutions.

On the roll of early Members are found the names of the *Sovereigns* of Belfast—Stewart Banks, John Brown, Edward May, M.P., and Thomas Ludford Stewart.

The *Clergy* are well represented by such names as James Bryson, Dr. Bruce, Sinclaire Kelburn, John Clarke, Patrick Vance, Edward Groves, Hugh O'Donnell. The last-named of these, it may be mentioned, was the highly respected and liberal-minded parish priest; and it is satisfactory to be able to record that the Belfast Society for Promoting Knowledge has always been a neutral meeting-ground for readers of all sects.

The *Medical* profession claims many distinguished members of the Society. Among others, in addition to those already named, may be mentioned Dr. John Campbell White, a man now almost forgotten in Belfast, but to whose powerful effort, already noted, to establish a FREE SCHOOL for the lower classes, the town owes a great deal of the present efficiency of its elementary school provision.

As a token of the troublesome times through which the country had recently passed, it may be mentioned that there is no record of any Meeting of the Society, or of a Committee of the Society, from the 19th of March, 1798, till the 9th of October following. This complete silence, for a period of over six months, tells its own tale, and is suggestive of the rigour of the martial law which then prevailed during this period of anarchy. As considerable changes had taken place in the *personnel* of the members during that eventful time, owing to the disorganised state of society, and the uncertainty and anxiety which existed, it was ordered, in October—

9th Oct., 1798. That a complete List of the present members of the Society be made out by the Secretary, and entered upon the minutes.

As this direction was duly complied with, we are enabled to give the names of the eighty-nine members who then constituted the Society, which will, no doubt, be of interest, even at this distant date :—

A Complete List of the Present Members of the Society, in alphabetical order, Belfast, 6th Dec., 1798 :—

Rev. J. Abernethy	Miss Clarke	John Gregg
John Alexander	Patk. Connor	Nichl. Grimshaw
Wm. Atkinson	Thos. Cruse	John Graham
Rob Bailie	Wm. Dinnen	Doctor Haliday
And. J. Barnett	Benj. Edwards	John Holmes
Thos. G. Bashford	Jas. Ferguson, Bclare	Rob Holmes
Thos. Bateson, Orangefield	Jas. Ferguson, Town	John Houston
Thos. Beggs	John Ferguson, Mill St.	Jas. Hyndman
David Bigger	Jno. S. Ferguson	John Ireland
Geo. Black, jun.	Jas. A. Ferris, Larne	Thos. B. Isaac, H.wood
Rob Bradshaw	Doctor Fuller	Miss M. Jones
Mrs. Isabella Brown	Thos. Gelston	Fras. Jordan
Doctor Bruce	Rob Getty	George Joy
John Caldwell	Saml. Gibson	Henry Joy
Rob Callwell	Wm. Goyer	James Joy

Jas. Kirker	Wm. Owens	John Templeton
John Knox	Jas. Pinkerton	Wm. Tennent
Wm. Magee	Wm. Rainey	Joseph Thoburn
Rainey Maxwell	Christopher Salmon	Henry J. Tomb
Wm. Moffet	Captain Scott	John Turnley
Jas. Munfoad	John Scott, Carrick	Alexr. Turnley
Richd. Murdock	Robert Simms	Revd. Pat. Vance
Jas. M'Adam	Wm. Simms	Rob Wallace
Saml. M'Comb	John Sinclaire	Geo. Wells
Edwd. M'Cormick	Wm. Sinclaire	Jas. Whittle
John M'Cracken	Hon. C. Skeffington	Dr. Wilson, N.ards
John M'Crum	Saml. Smith	Dr. Wilson, Parkgate
Dr. M'Donnell	Hamilton Steele	Walter Wilson
Thos. M'Donnell	Dr. Stephenson	John Younghusband
Gilbert M'Ilveen, jun	Rob Telfair	

PART II.

ANNALS OF THE SOCIETY

From 1800-1888.

HAVING recorded in some detail the circumstances connected with the origin of the Belfast Library and Society for Promoting Knowledge, and its progress during the early years of its existence, we shall now present a brief summary, under each year, of its proceedings, from the year 1801 to the present time.

1801.

President—Dr. Bruce. *Vice-President*—John Holmes. *Secretary*—James Munfoad. *Committee*[1]—John H. Houston, Dr. S. M. Stephenson, Dr. Wm. Haliday, Rob Telfair,[2] Gilbert M'Ilveen, Thos. M'Donnell, Jno. S. Ferguson, Robert Callwell, Christopher Salmon,[3] James M'Cleery,[4] Rev. W. St. John Smyth.[5]

During the year the President was directed—

22nd Oct. To write to Mr. John Caldwell, of New York, acknowledging the receipt of sundry skins, of which he had made a present to the Society.

In this year also the thanks of the Society, as already recorded, were sent to Dr. Forster, of Hamburg, for his gift of fossils and minerals ; and the President was requested "to obtain a specimen of the Wicklow gold for Mr. Forster, agreeable to his request." Before, however, this resolution could be carried out, intelligence arrived of the death of Loth Dr. Forster and his son.

1802.

On the 4th February is the following entry :—

4th Feb. This day being the usual day for electing President, Vice-President, and Secretary for the year ensuing, and Committee for three months, the Society was summoned to attend at seven o'clock ; but, as the evening

---

(1). The Committees were elected for three months at this period. It would be tedious to give the names at each election. The names of the then existing Committee will, however, be given at the commencement of each period of ten years. A complete list of Members of Committee from the commencement will be found in the Appendix.

(2). Writing-master at the Belfast Academy, and, although deprived of two fingers on the right hand, he was an excellent writer and a great teacher. Telfair Street was named after him or his son.

(3). A Custom-house officer, who, on retiring, had a purse containing 100 guineas presented to him by the merchants of the town.

(4). Lagan Canal Navigation Office.

(5). Curate at St. Ann's.

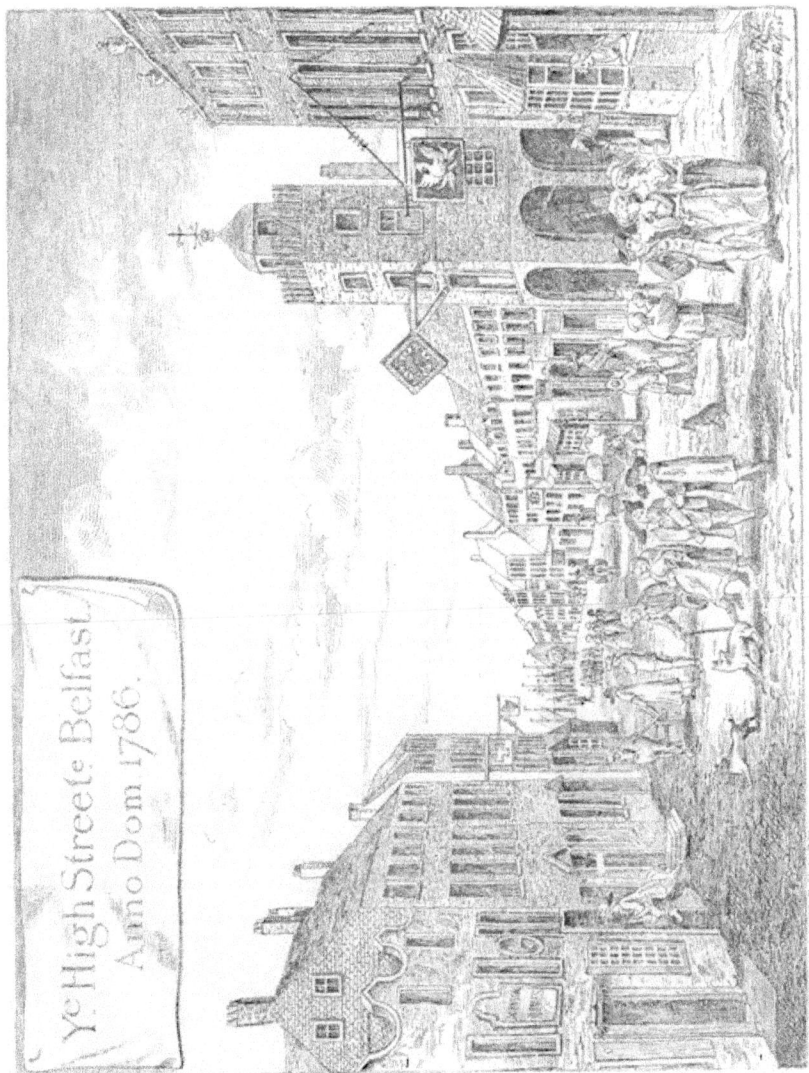
Ye High Streete Belfast. Anno Dom 1786.

4th Feb., 1802. was very stormy, few members attended. It was, therefore, thought best by the few members present to postpone the electing of Officers and Committee to a future day.

The ballot took place at the next meeting, when the President, Vice-President, Secretary, and most of the old Committee were re-elected.

Mr. Mumfoad, however, only held his post till April, when Mr. Thomas M'Donnell was appointed to succeed him.

At the same meeting the Society granted the use of their new room at the Linen Hall—"when they got possession of it"—to the Literary Society to hold their meetings in.

Dr. Bruce, Mr. Templeton, and Dr. Saml. Smith Thomson were instructed to revise the Laws of the Society, and to form a new Catalogue of the Books and Inventory of the Cabinet, with power to call in the Books and remove the property of the Society to the New Library.

It was also decided to pay the Librarian £20 a year after the Library be removed.

At the next meeting it was reported—

6th May. That the late Dr. Haliday had transferred to this Society a Legacy of Books bequeathed to him by the late Mr. Dalway. That amongst the books are the Irish Statutes at Large from 1310 till 1762, with an Index, and the Commons' Journals down to 1764, with Appendix and Index—in all, 24 Folio volumes.

The first Committee meeting in the new Library[1] was held 27th of May, when it was reported that Mr. Hill Wilson had lent the Society a set of the French Encyclopédie, for which a receipt was handed him. The first meeting of the Society at large at the Linen Hall took place on June 3rd—twenty-four members being present.

Mr. James Sloan was elected Librarian, and gave security in £100. Mr. T. M'Donnell agreed to continue as Secretary, provided he be exempt from attendance at the meetings. This was allowed, and Mr. G. M'Ilveen offered his services as substitute.

The complete list of the Rules of the Society, as revised and approved by the Sub-Committee, was ordered to be entered upon the Minutes.

Dr. Haliday's gift of books was completed during the year, and contained many valuable works in addition to the Irish Statutes. Several other gifts were received for the Museum and Library; and, as a proof of the progress which the Library had made, it may be noted that during the year several duplicate volumes were sold.

In August, a proposal to reduce the quorum of Committees from seven to five, owing to the frequent difficulty in getting together the larger number, was passed, but, on being submitted for confirmation at next meeting, was negatived.

The following letter, dated October 16th, from Mr. Thomas Robinson,[2] is interesting:—

(1). It is curious that the Secretary heads the Minutes of this meeting—"Book Society, White Linen Hall, 27th May, 1802."

(2). This gentleman was father to the late Dr. Romney Robinson, Irish Astronomer Royal at Armagh. A picture of his (probably the one referred to) is in the Board Room of the Harbour Commissioners. It contains portraits of several of the gentlemen mentioned in these pages, as also that of himself and his son Romney.

18th Oct., 1802. GENTLEMEN,—Being engaged in painting a picture of Shipping, and being unable to procure any accurate representation of Ships to assist me in some parts which I have not had an opportunity of seeing, I request the Committee would allow me for a few days Alderman Boydell's Collection of Prints. I will be accountable for any damage, and will consider myself under particular obligations to the Belfast Society for Promoting Knowledge.—Your Humble Servant, THOS. ROBINSON.
Belfast, 16th Oct., 1802.

Permission was given to Mr. Robinson to have the volume for one week.

1803.

President—Dr. Bruce. *Vice-President*—Dr. Stephenson. *Secretary*—Thos. M'Donnell.

It is considered that the following entry will be of interest on account of the prices attached to the Books.

On January 13th it was resolved—

13th Jan. That the Chairman shall write to our President, now in Dublin, to purchase for this Society, out of the Library of the late Lord Chancellor,[1] the following books, if to be had at or under the limits annexed to each work :—

No. 139	Stedman's Description of Surinam	...	2	Guineas
„ 140	Symes' Embassy to Æva	... ...	1½	„
„ 141	Vancouver's Voyage	... ...	5½	„
„ 227	State Trials. 11 Vols. ...	... ...	11	„
„ 231	Ware's Works. 2 „ ...	... ...	4	„

At the General Meeting it was decided that Honorary Members should have the use of the Library, subject to the rules ; and it was stated that at that date the Honorary Members of the Society were Alderman John Boydell, John M'Coughtry, and Job Rider.

It was also determined—

13th Jan. That in the future every gentleman who proposes a member shall pay the admission money at the time he proposes him. The money to be returned in case the candidate is not admitted.

At the next meeting, Dr. Thomson's offer of *Bayle's Dictionary*, at four guineas, was accepted.

The three Inspectors appointed in May were Dr. Thomson, Dr. Haliday, and Mr. John Templeton. They were directed, in addition to their ordinary duties, to have an Appendix to the Catalogue printed.

For three months of this year it was decided to keep the Library open in the evenings from 6 to 8, with an allowance of 2½ guineas to the Librarian for this additional attendance.

A large number of volumes were purchased during the summer at the sale of the late Mr. Warren's Library—about forty-five interesting works in all, for which the sum of £11 12s. 1½d. was paid.

1804.

President—Dr. Bruce. *Vice-President*—Dr. Stephenson. *Secretary*—Thos. M'Donnell.

---

(1). This was the Earl of Clare, the first Irishman who held the office.

View of Belfast from Old Paper

ll in 1805. Population, 22,000.

1st Mar., 1804. On the application of the Literary Society of this place—Resolved—That they be allowed the use of the Drawers in our Bookcases for specimens of Fossils, &c.

At the sale of Mr. Maxwell's books in March, purchases to the amount of £12 0s. 6d. were made by the Society.

3rd May. The President reported that he had called upon Mr. May, their representative in Parliament, to try and obtain through him copies of the Acts of the Imperial Parliament since the Union (1800). That Mr. May said the Society were welcome to his own copies, which were lying in London. Ordered—That the Secretary endeavour to get an order from Mr. May to hand over to our agent in London the said copies, so that the Books might be forwarded to the Society.

On July 5th the Inspectors presented a report, showing that a considerable number of books were missing; while others were in a "bad plight," or needed repair. The Secretary was ordered to call upon one member for the amount of *Beckman's Inventions.*

Mr. Jamieson, the London agent of the Society, was paid £10 6s. 0d., British, for a pair of globes.

The following Minute appears under date December 6th :—

6th Dec. Resolved—That the Chairman shall write to Mr. Abernethy, informing him that his conduct has given offence to many members of this Society; and that, unless he discontinues his personal attendance at the Library, a meeting will be called for the special purpose of considering the propriety of expelling him.

1805.

President—Dr. Bruce. *Vice-President*—Dr. Stephenson. *Secretary*—Thos. M'Donnell.

A list of the property of the Society, not included in the Catalogue, is presented as follows :—

6th June. 3 Tables, 2 Reading Desks, 12 Chairs, 1 Step Ladder, 1 Pair of Globes and Covers, a Cabinet of Fossils, 6 Maps on Rollers, an Air Pump and its Barometer, a Rain Gauge and Case, Wedgwood's Pyrometer, 2 Barometers, and 2 Thermometers.

DRAWERS :—

(A)—Several Curiosities from America.
(B and C)—Fossils and Lavas from Italy.
(D)—Natural Curiosities of Ireland.
(E)—Broken—to be Repaired.
(F)—American Curiosities of the Literary Society.
(G)—Botanic Fasciculi.
Maps.

6th June, 1805.   Resolved—Mr. Robinson having requested permission to finish his painting in the Library, permission is granted for him to finish the same during Library hours.

1st Aug.   Resolved—That the President do apply, in the most respectful manner, in the name of the Society, to the Rev. Rob. Trail, to request that he will favour the Society with some articles of Irish Antiquity, which we understand he is disposed to deposit with some public Literary Body.

Dr. Trail responded to this request by presenting an Urn and Bones, and an Ancient Cross found in Scotland.

5th Sept.   Dr. Bruce, Dr. Thomson, and Mr. M'Adam were appointed to examine some specimens of stone from the Giant's Causeway which have been brought to town, with discretionary power to purchase them.

The specimens were purchased for one guinea.

5th Sept.   Resolved—That the permission formerly given to Mr. Robinson for painting in the Library be limited to the 1st of November next; and Dr. Bruce is requested to inform Mr. Robinson of this resolution.

A Committee, appointed in August to select such books as (on account of their value, size, or for other special reasons) were not to be lent out of the Library, reported in September, with the following List of Works to be so excluded :—

5th Sept.

Bengal Atlas	Dickson's Botanic Fasciculi and
General Atlas	Hortus Siccus. Smith's Do.
Beaufort's Memoir and Map	Donovan's Insects
Boydell's Plates	Drury's Illustrations
Camden's Britannia	Irish Bible
Cook's 2nd & 3rd Voyages. 5 vols.	Johnson's Dictionary
4th edition.	Latham's Synopsis
D'Anville's Atlas	Martin's Flora Rustica
Plates of Staunton's China	Curtis' Botanic Magazine
Charts of all Kinds	Philosophical Transactions

1806.

President—Dr. Bruce. *Vice-President*—Dr. Stephenson. *Secretary*—Thos. M'Donnell.

A sub-committee was appointed to prepare a further Appendix to the Catalogue. On March 6th the Balance in the hands of the Secretary was £115 18s. 10d.

6th Mar.   Resolved—That such Books as are marked in the Catalogue with an asterisk shall not be lent without the consent of the Committee, and that the Cyclopædia shall not, on any account, be lent out of the Library.

The chief business of the year was a careful revision of the books, the preparation of the appendix, and the purchase of several important new works.

In October we find that Dr. Stephenson was allowed to have the pyrometer for one month ; also that permission was occasionally granted for the loan of books or maps on the special list before referred to.

1807.

President—Dr. Bruce. *Vice-President*—Dr. Stephenson. *Secretary*—Thos. M'Donnell.

In the Report of the Inspectors, made June 4th, it was stated, among other things, that the Secretary's accounts were correct, but they showed arrears due to the amount of £108 12s. 7½d. They were, therefore, requested—

4th June. To take the trouble of making personal application to the members in arrears for the payment of the same.

At the same meeting the Librarian was ordered to replace a missing volume, and the Inspectors were requested to settle with another member for a book lost by him.

The difficulty of securing as large a quorum as seven regularly at the meetings of the Committee once more occupied the attention of the Society. A second proposal to reduce the quorum to five had been rejected. It was now proposed—with a view to secure a quorum on all occasions—to increase the number of members of the Committee to twenty. This, however, was rejected ; and the following curious compromise, proposed by the President, was agreed upon :—

6th Aug. That whenever a Quorum of the Committee cannot be obtained, it shall be in the power of the Chairman or Senior Member to invite as many of those members of the Society who shall first appear as may be necessary to make a Quorum, to sit as Members of the Committee for that day, provided there be Four Members of the Committee present before such invitation be given.

3rd Sept. Resolved—That the Chamber of Commerce[1] shall have permission to lodge their Volumes of Acts of Parliaments in the Library, for the purpose of their Members referring to them occasionally in the Library hours.

1808.

President—Dr. Bruce. *Vice-President*—Dr. Stephenson. *Secretary*—Jas. Munfoad.

The thanks of the Society were voted to the late Secretary.

On January 7th of this year, Mr. Templeton, Mr. Callwell, and Dr. Haliday were appointed a sub-committee to apply to the Linen Hall Committee for an increase in their room space for books, &c. ; and, at a later meeting, Dr. Haliday reported that the lobby of the Library could be got "so as to enlarge the number of our bookcases." The new space was immediately occupied, and the Librarian's salary raised to Thirty Guineas for all his duties and attendance.

It was also decided to have the open part of the landing at the top of the stairs enclosed as a closet for the use of the Library.

---

(1). Established 1800, to guard the mercantile interest of the town, and to act as arbitrators. President this year, Wm. Sinclaire ; Vice-President, Narcissus Batt ; with Council of Fifteen Members.

D

13th Oct., 1808.   The Catalogue of Lord Dungannon's Library, to be sold by auction, at Belvoir, on the 24th inst., was examined, and several books marked, which the Committee thinks should be purchased for the Library, if they can be got at a moderate price. Dr. Haliday and Robert Callwell are appointed to attend there, and make the purchases.

It appears that 91 vols. were secured for the Library at this sale.

1809.

President—Dr. Bruce. *Vice-President*—Dr. Stephenson. *Secretary*—Jas. Munfoad.

Among the books purchased this year were—

    Lay of the Last Minstrel...   ..   ...   9s. 9d.
    Marmion ...   .   13s. 0d.

There was little business beyond routine transacted during the year.

1810.

President—Dr. Bruce. *Vice-President*—Dr. Stephenson. *Secretary and Treasurer*—Jas. Munfoad.

Committee :—

Dr. Samuel S. Thomson[1]	Rev. Edward Groves[2]	Dr. Marshall[4]
Robert Callwell	John S. Ferguson	Rainey Maxwell
Wm. Tennent	Rev. W. St. John Smith[3]	James M'Adam[5]
John Templeton	James M'Cleery	

The Inspectors' report this year specially commended the care exercised by the Librarian, and pointed out that not a single book had been lost since last inspection.

The following Minutes show that the compromise arrived at with regard to the attendance at Committee meetings had by no means settled the difficulty complained of :—

4th Oct.   That whereas great inconvenience and delay have arisen from the non-attendance of members of Committee, the addition made to Rule XV. on the 15th of Feb., 1807, be repealed, and that the following additions shall be made :—

And should no Quorum be thus obtained half an hour after the regular time of meeting, then the members present, provided the President, Vice-President, or Secretary be one of the number, shall be empowered to do the business allotted to the Committee.

But at the general meeting of the Society in December—which was only attended by members of the Committee—this proposal was negatived, thus leaving the vexed question as unsettled as ever.

1811.

President—Dr. Bruce. *Vice-President*—Dr. Stephenson. *Secretary and Treasurer*—Jas. Munfoad.

---

(1). A well known Physician, and for many years an active Member of the Anacreontic Society.
(2). Incumbent of Holywood.
(3). Curate of St. Ann's, afterwards Rector of Ballyphilip, and Chancellor of Down.
(4). Grandfather of the Right Hon. A. M. Porter, now Master of the Rolls in Ireland.
(5). Father of Robt. M'Adam, Esq., now and for many years a valuable Member of Committee.

7th Feb., 1811.   Resolved—That the Committee be empowered to lend any single volumes marked thus (†) in the catalogue which may have been published within Five Years past, on the person borrowing (being a Subscriber) depositing treble its value, and that it shall be returned, uninjured, in Four Weeks from the date of its being lent.

A further Appendix to the Catalogue was ordered—and was in due time printed by D. & S. Lyons—consisting of ten pages.

Complaints having been made of the length of time required, under the present system, for the delivery of books ordered from London through the Belfast booksellers, it was resolved in September—

5th Sept.   That for three months ensuing all orders for books shall be given by our Secretary to Messrs. Gilbert & Hodges, Dame Street, Dublin, to be by them purchased and forwarded to us.

The following resolution was passed with a view of lessening the inconvenience caused by the frequent want of a quorum at Committee meetings:—

3rd Oct.   Resolved—That the following clause be added to Rule XXI. :—But should the decision of the Committee respecting any book which may have been proposed be delayed by the non-attendance of the members beyond the third Monthly Meeting subsequent to its proposal, then in such case the Secretary may be empowered to order such Book upon a written requisition signed by ten members.

On 17th October a list of 49 volumes was presented, and purchased from Mr. C. Lewis.

1812.

President—Dr. Bruce.   *Vice-President*—Dr. Stephenson.   *Secretary and Treasurer*—Jas. Munfoad.

2nd Jan.   John Templeton, Dr. S. S. Thomson, and Henry Joy gave in their plan by which the Books in the Library may be better arranged, and that it may be more easily known, when any book is wanted, whether it is or is not in the Library, at the time.

This plan is approven, and ordered to be carried into execution.

During this year several members, whose subscriptions were in arrear, were threatened with expulsion from the Society, and a list of such defaulters upon the minutes shows that some were as much as five years behind in their payments. It is not recorded whether extreme measures were taken with the defaulters; but the following resolution reads as if some names at any rate had been removed from the list :—

7th May.   That from particular circumstances, not to be drawn into precedent, the Rev. Mr. O'Beirne[1] be now re-admitted as a Member on paying the Subscription for the present Year from this date.

---

(1). Afterwards Classical Master for the Academical Institution.

On the 4th June is entered a list of some 90 volumes purchased at Stockdale's auction in the Exchange. Several of these were valuable works, and were marked in the list with an asterisk as books not to be lent out without special permission.

The rapid growth of the Library necessitated a further extension of the accommodation, and in July it was resolved—

2nd July. That the recommendation of the Inspectors to have the east end of the inner room fitted up for books be adopted.

At the same meeting a further Appendix was ordered, to include the recent acquisitions of the Library, and Dr. Stephenson was appointed to examine the Museum and Philosophical Apparatus, and report upon their state.

The Inspectors of the Library reported satisfactorily during the year, and in August Dr. Stephenson made the following report as to the Museum :—

6th Aug. I examined the Fossils, and find them in the Cabinet agreeable to the original List, and other Fossils in drawers belonging to the "Literary Society," without Lists.

Parts of the columns of the Giant's Causeway are in the Library, so are the globes, Wedgwood's pyrometer, and an air-pump.

P.S.—3 Tables, 12 Chairs, a Rain Gauge, a Step-ladder, 2 Rubbers, 2 Basons and 1 Stand, a Jug, and a Cup for Soap; 2 Thermometers, 2 Barometers, 6 Maps—1 of Ireland, 1 County Antrim, 1 Lough Neagh, a Chart of the Levant, a Chart of Biography, and one of History.

The Zebra Skins should be washed to prevent or kill vermin.

S. M. STEPHENSON.

1st Oct. The staircase and lobby are ordered to be enclosed, under the superintendence of Mr. Jno. Templeton.

At this time, it appears, the Society was procuring its books—some through the Post Office, some from Gilbert & Hodges of Dublin, and others in Belfast, through Samuel Archer and Robert Callwell.

1813.

President—Dr. Bruce. *Vice-President*—Dr. William Drennan.[1] *Secretary and Treasurer*—Jas. Munfoad.

7th Jan. The Librarian is ordered to keep the doors of the shelves where the books are placed 'locked' during the time there is any public meeting held in the Rooms, and not to open them to lend Books until such meeting may be adjourned.

The other business of the year was wholly of a routine character.

---

(1). Physician; son of the Rev. Thos. Drennan, of the First Presbyterian Church, Belfast; author of several works; and father of our present highly respected Vice-President, John S. Drennan, Esq., M.D.

1814.

President—Dr. Bruce. *Vice-President*—Dr. Stephenson. *Secretary and Treasurer*—Jas. Munfoad.

This year was notable for the publication of a New Catalogue of the Books, of which, in March, 250 copies were brought from the printer, Mr. Alex. Mackay, of the *News-Letter* Office, at the cost of £16 1s. 4d. This Catalogue is printed on one side of the leaf only, and the 35 rules of the Society are prefixed, headed by the following declaration :—

> That the object of this Society is the collection of a Library, a Philo-sophical Apparatus, and a Cabinet of Natural History.
>
> ☞ Donations of Books, Instruments, Specimens of Minerals, Ani-mals or Plants, Statues, Paintings, and Models of Machines will be thank-fully acknowledged.
>
> Charts of all kinds, and Books marked thus (†), except as under Rule XXXIII., cannot be lent out of the Library. Books marked thus (*) cannot be lent without consent of the Committee.

At the end of the Catalogue is a list of "broken sets," with the following notice :—

> It is requested that the subscribers will make diligent inquiry after the volumes wanting to complete the above-mentioned Broken Sets, and give the earliest notice to the Librarian, in order that they may be procured.

7th July.   Thursday, the 7th July, being the day appointed for thanksgiving, the Committee was not summoned.[1]

1815.

President—Dr. Bruce. *Vice-President*—Dr. Stephenson. *Secretary and Treasurer*—Jas. Munfoad.

The growing popularity of the Library at this time is marked by the following Minute on the first meeting of the year :—

5th Jan.   Resolved—That Gentlemen who were only temporary residents in the town may be admitted to read in the Library by consent of the Com-mittee.

This permission was subsequently limited to a period of one month.

This year, owing to the erection of a cupola on the buildings of the Linen Hall, immediately over the Library, and to the consequent removal of the books into other rooms, the following notice was ordered to be inserted in the newspapers :—

5th Oct.   That, on account of the alterations now making in the Library, the Librarian is only to attend from 1 till 3 o'clock.

The following Minute points to the completion of this structure, which forms an appropriate termination to Donegall Place. (See frontispiece.)

---

[1]. This thanksgiving to the Almighty was for the restoration of the blessings of peace. It does not appear to have been publicly observed in Belfast ; but in London there was a grand and most imposing procession through the city to St. Paul's, the Duke of Wellington, who had recently returned from the Peninsular War, being the hero of the day.

7th Dec., 1815.　　The Librarian is ordered to have the books returned to the Library as soon as in his power, and lay them on the floor. The placing the books in the cases and making a class catalogue is to be under the direction of Mr. Templeton, Revd. Mr. Crolly,[1] and Mr. James Ferguson. The Librarian to be allowed two Guineas for his extra trouble.

In April appears the first financial statement of the affairs of the Society recorded on the Minutes, embracing the income and expenditure for the past seven years. It is as follows :—

6th April.

STATEMENT OF THE TREASURER'S A/C. WITH THE SOCIETY, COMMENCING 4TH APRIL, 1808, UP TO 1ST FEB., 1815.

1814					1808				
Dec. 31—To S. Archer and Jas. M'Cleery, since April, 1808...	£549	16	3½		Apl. 4—By Cash received from T. M'Donnell	...£106	13	3½	
,,　To Monthly Reviews, &c.	33	4	7½		By Subscriptions and Admissions	84	7	5½	
To New Books at Auctions	111	5	8½		1809 By ,, ,, ...	157	5	6	
To Old ,, ,, ...	48	0	8		1810 By ,, ,, ...	137	10	9¼	
To Gilbert & Hodges ...	51	5	0		1811 By ,, ,, ...	158	18	9½	
To Librn.'s Sal., Coals, and Cleaning ...	298	9	10		1812 By ,, ,, ...	191	13	10½	
To New Bookcases, &c...	71	18	7½		1813 By ,, ,, ...	173	6	11½	
1815					1814 By ,, ,, ...	166	9	0	
Jan. 10—To Librarian, due 31st Dec.	17	1	3		By Gain on Gold sold ..	0	13	0	
,,　To Sweeping Chimneys, &c.	0	16	8		By Cash Last Book ..	0	13	6	
To Magazines	1	0	0		1815				
Feb. 1—To Cash in hands... ...	68	12	3		Feb. 1—By Subscriptions and Admissions since 1st Jan.	73	18	9	
	£1251	10	11			£1251	10	11	

1816.

President—Dr. Bruce.　*Vice-President*—Dr. Stephenson.　*Secretary and Treasurer*—Jas. Munfoad.

Complaints appear to have been again made respecting the frequent long delays in the delivery of books ordered from London. It was not uncommon for parcels to be two or even three months in transit. At the December meeting the matter was brought under the notice of the Committee; and as the President was at that time in Dublin, he was by resolution requested to make application to such booksellers as he might think competent to supply the Library on the best terms.

Dr. Bruce subsequently reported that Mr. Milliken, of Dublin, offered to supply the books ordered at London prices, and would have them sent to Belfast, free of expense, expeditiously. It was thereupon resolved that all books which could not be procured in Belfast should in future be ordered through Mr. Milliken.

(1). Afterwards Doctor Crolly, the Roman Catholic Bishop of the Diocese, and subsequently Primate.

1817.

President—Dr. Stephenson.   *Vice-President*—James Ferguson.   *Secretary*—Jas. Munfoad.

6th Feb.   The Rev. Dr. Bruce, who had filled the situation of President for the period of nineteen years by annual elections, signified his intention not to accept the position on the present occasion, as he found it was not in his power to attend the meetings of the Society.

The Society received this information with regret, and voted their thanks to Dr. Bruce for the services he had rendered to it, and for the great attention he had paid to their interests and welfare for a series of twenty-five years, having been elected a member in the year 1792.

At the same meeting Mr. Munfoad, in accepting re-appointment, intimated his intention of resigning his post in May. Fortunately, however, he appears to have reconsidered the matter, and the Society continued to have the benefit of his active assistance and advice for many years.

6th Mar.   The stuffed skin of a Rattle Snake having been received from Mr. Magwood, of Charleston, South Carolina, through Cunningham Greg, Esq. ; ordered—That our President write a letter to Mr. Greg, and request he will return the thanks of the Society to Mr. Magwood for his Present.

5th June.   It was ordered that a Book be provided and kept in the Library for entering the names of those who are introduced by Subscribers for the purpose of reading there.

During the year a list of forty-three members, whose subscriptions were in arrear, was presented. Of these, eighteen were in arrears for two or three years.

The Society received a gratifying recognition of its importance in the summer of this year from the authorities, which is thus recorded:—

7th Aug.   The Secretary reported that on the application of their late President, the Rev. Dr. Bruce, the Society had received as a gift from the Commissioners of the Public Records, viz. :—The Reports and Proceedings of the Commissioners of Public Records of Ireland from 1810 to 1815, Folio. Dr. Stephenson, our present President, is requested to wait upon Dr. Bruce and return him the thanks of the Society for his trouble in obtaining this book, and request him to return the thanks of the Society to the Commissioners for their valuable Present.

With regard to this new acquisition, the following instruction was recorded:—

NOTE.—This Book is not to be given out of the Library to any person whatever.

The Library already appears to have been outgrowing its lately extended premises, and the matter, with suggestions, was laid before the Society in a letter from Dr. Drennan. It was decided, however, that for the present it was "not requisite to make any alterations "in the Library or its Furniture."

At the meeting of 4th September, the Marchioness of Donegall was proposed as a member by Dr. Thomson, and immediately elected.

At the same meeting an Appendix to the Catalogue was ordered to be printed, and Mr. Templeton was requested to prepare the manuscript.

A request by the Rev. Samuel Hanna,[1] Professor of Divinity to the Presbyterian students, to be allowed six books at a time, from November to May, for the use of his students, was considered by the Society, and on September 4th was rejected.

It was also resolved at the same meeting—

4th Sept.   That in future the Secretary post up in the Library, two weeks before next meeting, the names of persons to be Balloted for admission, and also such propositions as may require to be confirmed.

This regulation was soon afterwards altered from two weeks to seven days' notice.

The Society suffered a loss at the close of the year in the death of the Librarian, Mr. James Sloan, who had filled the office for fifteen years. It was resolved to advertise for a successor, Mr. Sloan's son, Robert, being meanwhile entrusted with the duties.

It was resolved at the same time that the Library in future should remain open from 11 till 4, and in the summer months from 6 till 8 in the evening.

And at a later meeting it was decided that the Librarian, in addition to his other duties, should collect the subscriptions.

The election of Librarian took place on December 4th—present, 66 members—when Robert Sloan received 33 votes, and was declared duly elected.

The following Minute occurs on October 2nd:—

2nd Oct.   That the Resolution passed on the previous 7th August to allow Members to have any of the Five last Years of the Philosophical Transactions, with leave of the Committee, be now confirmed.

It is worth recalling the fact that for the loan of one volume (that of 1777) of these Transactions, Mr. Job Rider had, in 1794, been called upon to give a promissory note for £100.

1818.

President—Dr. Stephenson.   *Vice-President*—James Ferguson.   *Secretary and Treasurer*—Jas. Munfoad.

At the meeting of the 4th December, Mr. Robert Callwell had been requested to apply for, and if possible obtain, the Votes of the House of Commons for the Library. It would appear that this application was successfully made, as it was ordered—

5th Mar.   That the Votes of the House of Commons be left with the News Room at Two Guineas per annum, and the Reports, &c., &c., to remain with the Library at Eight Guineas.

It was found necessary during the year to replace the old thermometers and barometers which had been among the first of the "Philosophical Apparatus" acquired by

(1). Afterwards the Rev. Samuel Hanna, D.D.; was Minister for many years in Rosemary Street, and was regarded as a leading man of the Church at a critical time.

the Society at the time of its formation. The new purchases were made through Mr. Wm. Sloan, a member of the Society, and are recorded as follows:—

5th Feb. To Wm. Sloan, for a Barometer and 2 Thermometers, £12 15s. od. English, or £13 16s. 3d. Irish, deducting 5 per cent. for prompt payment ; also freight and charges from London, when the amount can be ascertained.

The old barometer was subsequently sold to the Librarian for one guinea.

The new Appendix to the Catalogue, printed by A. Mackay, and consisting of twelve pages, was laid on the table in April.

The severe illness of the Librarian, necessitating his absence during part of the summer, was a cause of considerable inconvenience to the Committee and readers ; and on September 10th it was resolved—

10th Sept. That the Library be open to give out and take in books on Tuesday, the 15th inst.; on Thursday, the 17th inst. ; and on every succeeding Thursday, from 10 till 12 o'clock, until the Librarian is able to resume his duty ; and that the Members of the Committee will attend during that time to do the requisite Work. Resolved, further—That Notice of the above resolution be inserted once in each of the public papers.

At the same meeting it was resolved to apply to the Committee of the Linen Hall for the room adjoining the Library on the west end ; and on November 14th Dr. Tennent reported—

14th Nov. That the Committee of the White Linen Hall have acceded to their request ; and Dr. Tennent and Mr. Joy were appointed to have a communication made between the rooms, and have bookcases put up, one on each side of the Fire Place.

1819.

President—Dr. Stephenson. *Vice-President*—James Ferguson. *Secretary and Treasurer*—Jas. Munfoad.

In January of this year, Dr. Tennent and Mr. Templeton were appointed to prepare a new Catalogue, with the direction that a Scientific Classification of the Books in the Library, as far as may be found practicable, be joined to the Alphabetical List.

At the February meeting the Committee was chosen by ballot for the usual period of six months. The inconveniences arising from these frequent elections had for some time been felt by the Society, and on March 4th it was resolved—

4th Mar. That the Committee who were chosen on the 4th Feb. last shall continue in Office for one Year, and that in future the Committee shall continue in Office during a Year, the same as the officers of the Society.

The Catalogue prepared by Dr. Tennent and Mr. Templeton was laid on the table on May 6th. It was printed by David Lyons, at a cost of £26 0s. 10d. for 250 copies. It contains 119 pages, comprising the Laws (15 pp.), The Alphabetical Catalogue (68 pp.), and the Classified Catalogue—arranged with Index Letters in the margin—(36 pp.). To the last named is added the following prefatory note :—

4th Mar., 1819.   In order to facilitate the finding of Books relating to particular sub-jects, the following classification of a few is submitted—viz. :—Biography, Dictionaries or Books of Reference, History, Memoirs, Travels, Voyages, and Science—comprehending Astronomy, Optics, Mathematics, Botany, Chemistry, Natural Philosophy, Natural History, Geology, Mineralogy, &c.

The request for assistance from members in completing " broken sets " was repeated ; and, in addition to the Catalogue of Books, a list of Maps, &c., was given, as follows :—

Antrim County	By Lendrick. 1780.
Churchman's Magnetic or Variation Chart.	1790.
Derry County	By G. V. Sampson. 1813.
Down Do.	By Williamson. 1810.
Ireland	By Beaufort. 1792.
Jamieson's Geographic Chart of Europe.	
Lough Neagh	By Williamson. 1785.
Poirson's Chart of the Levant.	
Spain and Portugal	By Mentelle. London, 1808.
United States of America...	By S. Lewis. 1815.
1 Pair of Globes, 20 inches diameter ...	By Bardin, London.

              The Terrestrial, to 1799.
              The Celestial, for 1800.
       A Cabinet, with a very fine Collection of Minerals.
       An Air-pump.

The Cataloguers appear to have experienced some difficulty in classifying a large number of the books, as will appear from the following curious MS. Table, inserted in the Linen Hall copy—(the only copy known)—of this interesting Catalogue :—

Folios.	4to.	8vo.	12mo.	18mo.	24mo.	
179	255	1115	201	3	1	Volumes not Classified.
5	30	95	2	0	0	Biography.
20	112	5	10	0	0	Dictionaries.
2	12	61	30	0	0	Memoirs.
6	56	143	12	0	0	Science.
2	67	104	17	0	0	Travels.
38	96	425	25	0	0	History.
0	33	48	0	0	0	Voyages.
252	661	1996	297	3	1	Sum of each.

Total Number of Volumes in the Catalogue, 3,210.

In June the following Minute was inserted :—

3rd June.   It being represented to the Committee by Mr. W. Sloan and Mr. James Thomson,[1] of the Academical Institution, that our Rain Gauge is altogether useless, it is, therefore, ordered that a new one be purchased. Mr. Sloan has promised to write to London for it.

The cost of the new Gauge is entered as £6 12s. 6d.

1820.

President—Dr. Stephenson.   *Vice-President*—Jas. Ferguson.   *Secretary and Treasurer*—Jas. Munfoad.

Committee :—

Wm. Tennent	Henry Joy	Dr. Thomson
Jno. Templeton	Robt. Callwell	Rev. W. Bruce
Dr. Tennent[2]	Dr. Robt. M'Cluney[4]	Wm. Sloan[6]
Dr. Knight[3]	W. H. Ferrar[5]	

With the exception of a resolution on July 6th, " that the *Philosophical Magazine* " be discontinued," the business of this year was chiefly of a routine character.

1821.

President—Dr. Stephenson.   *Vice-President*—James Ferguson.   *Secretary and Treasurer*—Jas. Munfoad.

On the 7th June the Librarian informed the Committee that he intended to leave the country for America in about twelve days, and desired, in consequence, to tender his resignation. Whereupon, it was ordered that an advertisement be inserted in the Newspaper for a Librarian on or before the 20th of the month.

The election of a Librarian appears to have been a ceremony of some solemnity in these days, and a short account of the present proceedings may be of interest. A day and hour having been fixed by the Committee, a summons to members to be in their places was inserted in all the newspapers. A preparatory meeting of the Committee was held upon the day appointed, when it was decided that, in order fairly to test the votes of the Society, a second Ballot should be held to determine which of the first two names chosen at the first Ballot should be elected ; and, further, that the Librarian appointed should give security, to be approved by the Committee, in a Bond of £100.

These preliminaries arranged, the Society assembled, at ten o'clock, on Saturday, June 23rd. Upwards of eighty members were present ; and the list given includes the

---

(1). James Thomson, Esq., LL.D., Prof. Mathematics, Collegiate Dept. Academical Institution—author of several valuable books—father of Sir Wm. Thomson, F.R.S., and of Professor James Thomson, Glasgow.

(2). Afterwards President of the Society, and father of Robt Jas. Tennent, Esq., at one time M.P. or Belfast, whose son Robert, of Rushpark, still keeps up the family connection with the Library.

(3). Wm. Knight, Esq., LL.D., Prof. Nat. Philosophy, Collegiate Dept. Academical Institution.

(4). Brother-in-law of the late George T. Mitchell, Esq., Director of the Belfast Bank.

(5). Resident Magistrate, &c. His daughter, widow of the late Robert Patterson, Esq., F.R.S., still survives.

(6). Father of John Sloan, Esq., Director of the Ulster Bank, and of Garnet Sloan, Esq.

names of almost all the prominent past and present members of Committee and other active supporters of the Society.

Before proceeding to the business of the day, a discussion arose on a claim put forward by Mr. Thomas M'Nair to a vote at the present election. Mr. M'Nair produced a letter addressed to the Librarian by his late brother-in-law, Mr. John Ireland, in 1818, stating that he had sold his interest in the Society to Mr. M'Nair, and requesting that the name of that gentleman should be entered in the books in place of his own. No such transfer appeared to have been made, and despite the fact that Mr. M'Nair had paid the subscription and used the Library for two years, his claim to a vote was considered insufficient, and, on being put to the vote, was disallowed.

The Society then proceeded to the business of the election of a Librarian in the room of Mr. Robert Sloan, who had resigned and gone abroad; previous to which, however, the Society declined to adopt the mode of ballot suggested by the Committee, and decided "that the Election be by Ballot in the usual way."

A ballot was then taken, with the following result :—

Wm. M'Clure	46 votes.
John Boyd	29 „
John M'Lester	8 „

Mr. M'Clure[1] was thereupon declared duly elected, and executed the necessary bond for the faithful discharge of his duties. The salary attaching to the post was £34 2s. 6d. per annum.

At the same meeting it was resolved—

23rd June. That Mr. Hy. Joy, with Dr. Drummond[2] and the Rev. Wm. Bruce, be appointed Inspectors to take an inventory of the books and other property of the Society in the Library, and, to enable them to do so, no books are to be lent out before Monday, the 9th July.

28th June. A letter was received from Mr. Morgan Jellet, a bookseller in town, offering to supply the Society with books as promptly and on as low terms as any other person either in Dublin or Belfast. It was resolved that Mr. Jellet's offer be accepted.

1822.

President—Dr. Stephenson. *Vice-President*—James Ferguson. *Secretary and Treasurer*—Jas. Munfoad.

An Appendix to the last Catalogue was ordered to be prepared by the Librarian early in the year. 250 copies were printed by Joseph Smyth, at a cost of £2 0s. 4d.

The arrangement with Mr. Jellet, the bookseller, appears to have been carried into effect. Among other works procured through him was Sismondi's *History of the Italian*

(1). Mr. M'Clure—brother of Sir Thomas M'Clure, Bart.—became subsequently a well known and highly respected Presbyterian Minister in Londonderry. In 1847 he was chosen unanimously to the office of Moderator of the General Assembly.
(2). W. H. Drummond, D.D., Minister for Fifteen Years of the Second Presbyterian Church, Belfast; author of a Poem on the Giant's Causeway, and other works.

Republics, 16 vols., 8vo, in French, charged £7 16s. od. When this work was ordered it was described in the proposal book as 11 vols., price £5 13s. 9d., and was thought to be translated into English. The Treasurer, with Mr. Callwell, was directed to apply to Mr. Jellet, and request him to take the work back on being allowed one pound sterling.

A relaxation of the rules was made this year in favour of Professor Hincks, President of the Belfast Natural History Society, who applied to have more books out at one time than were usually allowed to a subscriber. It was decided in his case that the Librarian should "permit him to have such books as he might require, agreeable to his request."

1823.

President—Dr. Stephenson. *Vice-President*—James Ferguson. *Secretary and Treasurer*—Jas. Munfoad.

A letter was received from Mr. Munfoad declining re-election, whereupon it was directed that a letter be sent to him, thanking him for his past long and useful services, and requesting him to continue in office. Mr. Munfoad, consequently, in deference to the wish of the Society, remained at his post.

The following Minute is of interest, as giving the names of a few specially popular works much in demand at the time :—

2nd Jan. The Librarian is directed to inform those persons who may apply for the following books that the time for keeping each Volume is for some time restricted to one week from this date, in order to accommodate subscribers —viz. :—"Voice from St. Helena," "Bracebridge Hall," "The Court of James the I. and The Court of Elizabeth," by Miss Aikin ; "The Sketch Book," and "Lights and Shadows of Scottish Life."

Complaints were once more raised as to the delay in procuring books ordered through the Society's Belfast agent ; and on April 3rd

3rd April. The Librarian was directed to inform Mr. Jellet, bookseller, "that all "orders for Books given to him, and not executed by him on or before the "next ensuing Committee Meeting after that at which the order was given, "shall be withdrawn."

The Society was again thrown into difficulty by the resignation of its Librarian. Mr. M'Clure gave notice, in June, that, on account of various engagements, he could not hold the office longer than the end of the second year.

The election of a successor took place on July 3rd, with pretty much the same ceremony as that described in 1821. As the names of all the members attending the meeting are recorded on the Minutes, it will be of interest to give the list here :—

3rd July. *Society Meeting, 3rd July, the following Members being present, to Elect by Ballot a Librarian.*

Dr. Stephenson	John Gregg	John Whittle
Jas. Ferguson	Thos. M'Nair	Adam M'Clean
Dr. Tennent	Rev. W. Hincks	John Templeton

3rd July, 1823.	John Ward	James Dunlop	Mr. Harvey
	Mr. Radcliff	J. Thomson	Drummond Anderson
	John Compton	Rev. J. Alexander	Richd. Thomson
	Dr. M'Gee	R. Neilson	Hugh Magill
	Lawson Annesley	Alex. Orr	And. M'Clean
	John Montgomery	R. Blackwell	W. H. Ferrar
	James Stuart	Dr. M'Donnell	Rev. Mr. Bland
	Rev. Dr. Bruce	John M'Adam	Rev. Mr. Bruce
	Wm. Suffern	Dr. Thomson	John S. Ferguson
	Wm. Clarke	Rev. Mr. M'Ewen	And. J. Barnett
	Mr. Guirini	Alex. Stewart	Rich. Ashmore
	Rev. Mr. Smith	Mr. Moore	Mr. Shannon
	Miss Patterson	Mr. C. Thomson	Hugh Montgomery
	John Gillis	Mr. P. Quin	Rev. Mr. Craig
	A. Kidd	Thos. Millar	A. K. Millar
	Rev. J. Reid	Wm. M'Clure	Jas. Munfoad

There were seven candidates for the vacant office, and the ballot resulted in the election of Mr. Alexander Henderson,[1] who gave the necessary bond.

The Library, as before, was closed to the 10th of the month, for an inspection of the books by Dr. Tennent and Mr. Templeton. A few were reported missing, and others unaccounted for.

The new Librarian, being at the time of his appointment a student, received permission from the Committee afterwards to attend Lectures at the Institution, for one hour in the day, for the present. The President, however, entered a protest against this arrangement.

1824.

President—Dr. Stephenson. *Vice-President*—Dr. Tennent. *Secretary and Treasurer* —Jas. Munfoad.

On January 1st, a letter was received from Dr. T. D. Hincks,[2] President of the Belfast Natural History Society, who had already presented several valuable works to the Library, requesting the loan of such specimens of Natural History as the Society was possessed of. The consideration of this request was deferred till the next Society meeting, when " the further consideration of the application was adjourned *sine die.*"

Power was given at the general meeting in February to light the Library with gas.[3]

Among the booksellers from whom books were procured during this year were Jellet, Archer, and Hodgson in Belfast, and Bohn in London.

A new Catalogue was ordered in May, under the superintendence of Dr. Tennent and Mr. Templeton, as before. It was printed by Joseph Smyth.

(1). Mr. Henderson afterwards became Presbyterian Minister at Lisburn, and subsequently a Military Chaplain.
(2). The Rev. Thos. Dix Hincks, LL.D., Professor of Hebrew, &c., Academical Institution, and father of the Rev. Dr. Edward Hincks, of Killyleagh, an eminent Oriental scholar, &c.
(3). This permission was withdrawn February, 1825.

The question of the Librarian's daily absence at lectures during Library hours was again raised in October, when a general meeting was summoned, by advertisement in the public papers, to consider the matter. Twenty-four members attended ; and, it having been ascertained that Mr. Henderson would require two hours to attend his different classes, it was resolved—

7th Oct. That Mr. Alex. Henderson, the Librarian, be permitted to attend the Lectures in the Institution, two hours each day, during Library hours, on his appointing a deputy who shall be approved by the Committee. Mr. Henderson is enjoined to summon the Committee the 21st inst., at 10 o'clock, to take into consideration the fitness of the person he intends to appoint his Deputy.

As there was no quorum of Committee on the 21st October, the matter was deferred until November 4th, when Mr. John Arnold[1] was accepted as a substitute for the Librarian every day during his absence, from 12 till 2 o'clock.

Among the books ordered this year was Chemnitz's *General System of Conchology.* 12 vols., Royal 4to. Price £30.

1825.

President—Dr. Stephenson. *Vice-President*—Dr. Robt. Tennent. *Secretary and Treasurer*—Jas. Munfoad.

It was resolved, on Feb. 3rd—

3rd Feb. That a sub-committee be appointed to enquire into the propriety of keeping the Library open longer, and at more convenient times, than at present, and at what additional expense it can be accomplished, and report ; also, the propriety of admitting persons to the use of the Library on their subscribing One Guinea per annum.

The idea of admitting subscribers at a guinea per annum, without entrance fee, had already been ventilated, and received strong support in the columns of the recently established *Northern Whig* newspaper. It met, however, with considerable opposition from the more conservative members of the Society ; so that on the day fixed for the consideration of the proposal (March 3rd) there was a large attendance. After considerable discussion, a motion for adjournment was carried, and the question consequently was shelved.

This appears to have occasioned a schism among the members, several of whom interested themselves in the promotion of the " New Belfast Library," which was started with a view to carry into effect the more popular measures declined by the old Society. The chief features of the New Library were that (1) the entrance fee was to be dispensed with, (2) the class of books selected was to be of a more popular character, (3) and the Library was to remain open till 11 p.m.

Despite of the support it received in the Press, and the disparagement cast upon the Society for Promoting Knowledge, the new venture does not appear to have been warmly taken up, and did not succeed.

---

(1). Afterwards woollendraper in High Street.

The new Catalogue, consisting of 72 pages, and dated this year, was laid on the table.

An exception to the rules, in favour of the Rev. James Seaton Reid, was made in May in the following terms :—

3rd May.   The Rev. J. S. Reid[1] is permitted to have as many books from the Library as he wants, not exceeding six books at one time. This permission is to continue for three months. Restricted books excepted.

Among the books received during the year was a copy of the Statutes of the Realm from Magna Charta to the End of the Reign of Queen Anne, 11 vols. folio ; presented to the Society from Government, through the Speaker of the House of Commons. This gratifying recognition of the importance of the Society was one of many tributes about this time to its rapid growth and the excellence of its management.

In November, the Librarian applied to appoint Mr. Solomon Love,[2] of Magherafelt, a divinity student, as his deputy during the hours in which he himself was absent at lectures. Mr. Love being considered a suitable young gentleman, his appointment was approved.

1826.

President—Dr. Stephenson.   *Vice-President*—Dr. Tennent.   *Secretary and Treasurer* —Jas. Munfoad.

The Society suffered a great loss this year in the death of Mr. John Templeton, whose active work on the Committee for upwards of thirty years had contributed largely to the improvement and extension of its position. He was one of the most regular as well as most industrious of the old members ; and it is at least singular that, with the exception of the following Minute, no mention is made on the records of the Society's loss :—

6th April.   Mrs. Templeton, of Malone, was elected in place of her husband, the late John Templeton.

The following Minute reminds us of the length of time still occupied in the transit of books from London to Belfast :—

2nd Nov.   Rev. W. Bruce informed the Committee that he expected a parcel of books from London, by the " Erin," in a few days.

The permission to the Librarian to attend lectures was again extended for six months ; and the Committee approved of the appointment of Mr. James M'Knight[3] as deputy during Mr. Henderson's daily absence.

On November 7th a meeting was held, agreeable to public notice, to consider the expediency of connecting the News Room in the Linen Hall with the Library of this Society. The proposal met with opposition, and, as on a former occasion, a motion for adjournment was carried, and thus disposed of the question for a while.

---

(1). Afterwards the Rev. James Seaton Reid, D.D., author of the *History of the Presbyterian Church in Ireland*, and Prof. of Ecclesiastical History in the University of Glasgow.
(2). Ordained Presbyterian Minister at Kenly, 1831.
(3). Afterwards the well-known Dr. M'Knight, of Londonderry.

1827.

President—Dr. Stephenson. *Vice-President*—Dr. Tennent. *Secretary and Treasurer* —Jas. Munfoad.

With the consent of the Committee, Mr. Robert Magill[1] was appointed the Librarian's deputy during the absence of the latter in Library hours at lectures.

The business of the year was wholly routine.

1828.

President—Dr. Robt. Tennent. *Vice-President*—Dr. Samuel Thomson. *Secretary and Treasurer*—Jas. Munfoad.

It was resolved unanimously—

7th Feb.   That the thanks of the Society now be returned to Dr. Stephenson for his great attention to the business of the Society during the time he filled the situation of President.

The books of the Society were insured this year with the Atlas Insurance Company for £2,000.

The method of procuring books again came under discussion, and it was resolved, in March—

6th Mar.   That if the Books can be obtained from a Bookseller in Town nearly on as low terms as from one in Dublin or London, that a preference be given to our townsman ; and that the Secretary be directed to write to the different Booksellers in town, requesting them to state on what terms they will supply the Society with such Books as may be ordered, and in what time they shall be delivered after receiving the order.

The Booksellers' proposals were received on April 3rd, as follows :—

Mr. Archer (including Periodicals), 12½ % off the Retail London Prices, or charge 10 % on the London Invoice, and pay all expense of Importation ; or 5 % off the London Invoice, the Society paying the expenses.

Mr. John Hodgson, for Books and Periodicals, 12½ % off the Retail London Prices.

Mr. Morgan Jellet, Books (excluding Periodicals), 12½ % off the London Retail Prices.

Mr. Phillips, Books (including Periodicals), 10 % off the London Retail Prices.

The terms offered by Mr. Archer and Mr. Hodgson being thus identical, a ballot was taken, and Mr. Hodgson was selected by 5 votes to 3.

4th Dec.   The Librarian is directed to lodge an appeal with the Commissioner of Police against the payment of £2 5s. od. Police Tax "applotted" on the Library Rooms.

---

(1). Mr. Magill was afterwards well known as an active promoter of Sunday School work.

E

The following list of books, purchased at a sale in town from a Liverpool house, is of interest, on account of the prices affixed :—

6th Mar.	Maurice's Hindoostan. 4 Vols., 4to. Bound	£4 4 0
	Hughes' Nat. History of Barbadoes. Folio	1 0 0
	Caulfield's Remarkable Characters. 4 Vols., 8vo	2 0 0
	Drake's Gleaner. 4 Vols., Royal 8vo. Boards	1 4 0
	Annales de l'Imprimerie des Alde par Renouard. 2 Vols. ...	0 12 0
	Nicholl's Life of Bowyer. 4to. Bound	0 10 0
	Ryan's Worthies of Ireland. 2 Vols., 8vo. Boards ...	0 15 0
	Oxley's Journals in New South Wales. 4to. Boards ...	0 18 0
	Swift's Works. By Sheridan. 19 Vols., 8vo	5 0 0
	Proctor's Journey Across the Cordillera of the Andes. 8vo.	
	Boards	0 6 0
		£16 9 0
	Abatement... ...	0 5 0
		£16 4 0

At the close of this year a full balance sheet of the affairs of the Society was entered on the Minutes, and continues to be thus recorded annually from this date.

The accounts of this year showed that there were 152 members of the Society, and that the Income was £213 19s. 3d., against Expenditure, £172 18s. 10½d.[1]

1829.

President—Dr. Tennent.   *Vice-President*—Dr. S. S. Thomson.   *Secretary and Treasurer*—Jas. Munfoad.

In April the Librarian, Mr. Henderson, signified his intention of retiring, and the Society met, with the usual formalities, on the 10th, to elect a successor. There were several candidates ; but, as one of these was the energetic and honoured Secretary of the Society, Mr. James Munfoad, he was unanimously elected, and hearty votes of thanks were accorded to him for his thirty years' labour on behalf of the Society, and also to the retiring Librarian for his attention to his duties while in office.

Mr. Munfoad, who, for twenty-one years, had discharged the double duties of Secretary and Treasurer, consented to retain the former of these offices in connection with his new duties, but resigned the office of Treasurer, which was thereupon given to Mr. Wm. Suffern.[2]

The new Librarian's tenure of office was of very brief duration, as his health broke down two months after his appointment, and made it necessary for him to resign. A fresh election shortly afterwards took place, when Alexander Neilson was appointed by 51 votes, against 41 cast for George M'Ewen.

(1.) A Table is given at the end showing for each year the Receipts and Expenditure, including the separate amount paid for books, till the present time.

(2.) Merchant, father of our respected townsman, John Suffern, Esq.

The following Library regulation was made in July:—

2nd July, 1829. That Members who reside five miles from Belfast will be allowed twice the number of books at one time more than those allowed to Members who reside within that distance.

An Appendix of 10 pages to the Catalogue of 1825 was prepared during the year, and printed by T. Mairs.

3rd Nov. Mr. M'Adam, Mr. Montgomery, and the Secretary were appointed to examine the articles of Natural History, supposed to be the property of the Literary Society,[1] along with Dr. Henry MacCormac,[2] who is to attend and assist on behalf of that Society.

Application was made to Sir Arthur Chichester, M.P. for the Borough, through Mr. W. Tennent and the Rev. Dr. Hincks, to know if he could procure for the Society copies of the Statutes as published.

The balance sheet for the year showed—Income, £213 19s. 3d.; Expenditure, £209 17s. 3½d. Number of Subscribers, 150.

1830.

President—Dr. Tennent. *Vice-President*—Dr. Thomson. *Treasurer*—Wm. Suffern. *Secretary*—James Munfoad.

Committee—

Wm. Tennent	John B. Shannon[4]	John Montgomery
Rev. Dr. T. D. Hincks	Robert M'Cluncy	Professor James Thomson
Robert Callwell	Rev. Wm. Bruce	Professor John Stevelly[6]
Drummond Anderson[3]	James M'Adam[5]	

We note the following interesting Minutes in reference to the management of the Library:—

4th Mar. Resolved—That any Members, on paying double the usual Subscription, shall be allowed to have double the usual number of Books, subject to Rule XI.

1st April. Dr. James Drummond[7] is permitted to have such Books on Natural History as he may have occasion to consult, he being employed in writing on that subject.

The Librarian was instructed not to lend any Books to any member who shall be known after this date to make any remarks, marginal notes, underline any passages, or otherwise abuse any Books belonging to this Library, until he receives further instructions from the Committee.

(1). Established in 1801, for reading Papers on Literary and Scientific subjects.

(2). An eminent physician and a voluminous writer; father of Sir Wm. MacCormac, M.D., &c., London.

(3). Proprietor of the *Belfast Commercial Chronicle*, and now represented by his son, John C. Anderson, Esq.

(4). Proprietor of Chemical Works, Ballymacarrett.

(5). An eminent local geologist, and one of the Founders of the Belfast Natural History and Philosophical Society.

(6). Professor of Natural Philosophy, Collegiate Dept. Academical Institution.

(7). James L. Drummond, Esq., M.D., Professor of Anatomy and Physiology, Collegiate Dept. Academical Institution.

In consequence of irregularities in the conduct of the Librarian, Alexander Neilson, an inquiry took place in the autumn, which led to his resignation and the consequent vacating of the office. His accounts were found to be £34 11s. 7d. in default.

The election of a successor took place on October 14th, previous to which it was settled that the salary of the Librarian should be £40 per annum, and security required for £200, and that the hours of attendance should be from 10 till 4 o'clock daily.

As the attendance of members on this occasion was unusually large, and the list of names shows many changes in the *personnel* of the Society, we give it here as it appears on the Minutes :—

14th Oct., 1830.   *Society Meeting, 14th October, 1830.*   *Present—*

Dr. Tennent	Dr. Drummond	R. F. Gordon
Dr. Thomson	A. G. Wilson	Sir Stephen May
Joseph Stevenson	D. Anderson	John Montgomery
Jas. Orr, M.D.	J. B. Shannon	Revd. Mr. Smith
Surgeon M'Cluney	Revd. Wm. Bruce	John S. Ferguson
Rob. Simms	Wm. Dillon	Revd. W. Finlay
John Lyle	Wm. Suffern	Alex. Mitchell
Clotworthy Dobbin	Wm. Burden	Mrs. Templeton
Mr. Sneyd	Lawson Annesley	Jas. Montgomery
Geo. Black	Rev. Dr. T. D. Hincks	Prof. Thomson
Thos. Duff	Charles Thomson	John Kane
James Reid	John Whittle	Miss M'Cance
Mr. Vance	Alex. Stewart	Surgeon Smylie
Counsellor Bradshaw	Revd. Mr. Porter	John Gillis
John Compton	Francis Turniey	Dr. M'Donnell
Thos. J. Andrews	Hugh Magill	Rob. Simms, jr.
Henry Rowan	Arthur Gamble	Arthur Crawford
John Black	Wm. Tennent	Revd. Jas. Seaton Reid
John Montgomery(Comber)	Revd. Dr. Hanna	James Lewis
Wm. Boyd	James Blair	Thos. Millar
Rob. Gamble	Jas. Ferguson	Dr. Murray
Revd. Dr. Bruce	John M'Adam	Lewis Reford
Rob. Joy	Wm. Cairns	Henry Joy
A. K. Miller	Counsellor M'Donnell	John Grattan
Wm. Turner	Wm. Ferguson	H. M'Comb
Rob. Moat	Henry J. Tomb	John Macartney
Surgeon Marshall	Rob. Montgomery	C. Trevor
Thos. M'Clure	John Andrews	J. D. Cosgrove
Valentine Whitla	Hugh Montgomery	Thos. Sinclair, jr.
Henry J. Holmes	Dr. Duncan	J. T. Tadd
Revd. Wm. Cairns	Robt. Callwell	Jas. M'Adam

MCDONNELL CROSS LAYD OLD CHURCH. R.W. 376.

The election on the present occasion was conducted on the principle that the person chosen must receive a majority of the votes of the members voting, for which purpose a second ballot might be taken, if necessary. The names of eleven candidates had been before the Committee, of which they selected seven for the consideration of the Society at large. At the first ballot, out of 93 votes given, George M'Ewen received 42; which not being a majority of members present, a second ballot was taken. On this occasion only 81 members voted, and, as Mr. M'Ewen again received 42 votes, as against 30 cast for Robert Blair and 9 for another candidate, he was declared duly elected.

The new mode of election appeared to have given satisfaction, as it was ordered—

14th Oct., 1830. That in the future appointments of Librarians, the rules adopted at this election should be the guide.

It was also resolved, with a view to the further improvement in the management of the Library—

7th Oct. That in future the Committee shall annually print and circulate among the Subscribers a statement of their accounts, with a list of the Subscribers who had paid for the Year; also, of the Books that had been added to the Library when under their charge.

The balance-sheet for 1830 showed—Receipts, £144 9s. 10d.; and Expenditure, £144 5s. 1½d. But this small balance was accounted for by the late Librarian's defalcations of £34 11s. 7d. For the same reason the number of subscribers only appears as 109, to which must be added 49 whose subscriptions were paid to Mr. Neilson, making 158 in all.

1831.

President—Dr. Tennent. *Vice-President*—Dr. S. S. Thomson. *Treasurer*—William Suffern. *Secretary*—James Munfoad.

The Society received during the year a valuable gift of about 100 works from Dr. Henry MacCormac, for which they voted thanks, and elected the donor an Honorary Member.

The business of the year was wholly routine.

The accounts showed—Receipts, £171 10s. 8½d.; Expenditure, £114 2s. 9d. Number of Subscribers, 155.

1832.

President—Dr. Tennent. *Vice-President*—Dr. T. D. Hincks. *Treasurer*—William Suffern. *Secretary*—Jas. Munfoad.

5th July. Resolved—That all Members of two years' standing be entitled to the use of two additional vols. at a time.

The balance-sheet for the year showed—Receipts, £231 17s. 5d.; Expenditure, £152 3s. 0d. Number of Subscribers, 145.

1833.

President—Dr. Tennent. *Vice-President*—Dr. T. D. Hincks. *Treasurer*—William Suffern. *Secretary*—Maurice Cross.[1]

---

[1]. Head Master of the Lancasterian School, Frederick Street, afterwards Secretary to the Commissioners of National Education, Dublin.

Mr. Munfoad, after about forty years' service, during the greater part of which he had acted as Secretary and Treasurer, resigned his position this year; and, though no special mention of the circumstance is made on the records, a glance through the Minute books, kept for so many years in his familiar handwriting, furnishes ample testimony to the value of his services to the Society, and the loss it sustained in his retirement.

At a meeting on July 4th is the following resolution relating to the transference of the scientific collections of the Society, which, in the rapid growth of the Library, had during recent years been somewhat overlooked :—

4th July.   That the Cabinet containing the Specimens of Natural History and other Scientific Articles belonging to this Society be given into the custody of the Belfast Natural History Society, and that a receipt be taken from the Society.

The balance sheet shows—Receipts, £279 1s. 7d.; Expenditure, £214 0s. 6d. Number of Subscribers, 156.

1834.

President—Dr. Tennent.   *Vice-President*—Rev. Dr. T. D. Hincks.   *Treasurer*—William Suffern.   *Secretary*—Maurice Cross.

The following resolution was adopted in February :—

6th Feb.   That whereas it has been the practice of this Society at large to elect the Librarian by Ballot, agreeable to Rule I., it is now deemed expedient that in future the Power of Election be confided to the Committee for the time being.

A general "call over" of the Library took place during the year, and a new Catalogue was prepared under the superintendence of Mr. Hodgson, bookseller, who, it would appear, was paid for his work.

In June, the following interesting letter was read at the meeting of the Committee :—

NEW BOSWELL COURT, LINCOLN'S INN,
April 17th, 1834.

5th June.   SIR,—It has been suggested to his Majestic's Commissioners in the Public Records Office of Great Britain, That it is expedient that copies of certain of the works published under their superintendence, forming upwards of 50 Vols. in large folio, should be deposited in a public Library in one of the principal Towns of the County of Antrim for the use of the said County—In consequence, I am instructed to request you will have the goodness to let the Commissioners know if there is any such Library in any town in the County of Antrim (not already possessed of the works in question), and when such Library was founded, How it is supported, What number of Volumes it contains, and to whom it is accessible; also, whether the contemplated Donation would be accepted.

I have the honour to be, Sir,

Your obt. humble Servant,

To the Clerk of the Peace   C. P. COOPER.
   for the County of Antrim, Ireland.

5th June.   Resolved—That the offer contained in the above letter be accepted, and that the Society be requested to communicate to S. Darcus, Esq., the information he requires.

In December, accordingly, the Society received 51 folio volumes from the Public Records Office.

The Society, although it had parted with its Scientific Museum, still continued to interest itself in atmospheric and meteorological observations ; and, during the year, a new Rain Gauge, " of the most approved construction," was procured, and the Barometers and Thermometers were taken by Professor Stevelly in order to have them adjusted by the Instruments of the British Association for the Advancement of Science ; and the Librarian was requested "to keep the Meteorological Register at 9 and 3 o'clock instead of 11 and 2."

At the meeting of June 5th, it was resolved, further—

5th June.   That it is the opinion of this Committee, That the Title by which this Society is at present designated shall be changed to the "Belfast Library."

At the last meeting of the year the old vexed question of the reduction of the quorum at Committee meetings once more came up, and was quietly disposed of in the following motion :—

4th Dec.   That the number of the quorum be changed from seven to five.

The balance sheet showed—Receipts, £262 19s. 7d. ; Expenditure, £232 17s. 2d. Number of Subscribers, 168.

1835.

President—Dr. Tennent. *Vice-President*—Rev. Dr. T. D. Hincks. *Treasurer*—Wm. Suffern. *Secretary*—Maurice Cross.

At the meeting on January 1st, it was resolved—

1st Jan.   That the Committee shall be authorised to appoint an orderly, and that Dr. Tennent shall be orderly for next month.

A new Catalogue was ordered, which was ready about the end of the year, and cost £16 13s. 6d. No copy appears now to be in existence.

In December it was resolved—

That Rule XIV. be printed in the New Catalogue, with the addition recommended by the Committee, viz. :—

The Society pledges itself to each individual member not to dissolve, or proceed to a division of the property, without the unanimous consent of two General Meetings convened for that purpose.

This rule not to prevent the exchange of imperfect copies for such as are perfect, or the sale of duplicates.

The balance sheet showed—Receipts, £215 10s. 5d. ; Expenditure, £155 8s. 1d. Number of Subscribers, 169.

1836.

President—Dr. Tennent. *Vice-President*—Rev. Dr. T. D. Hincks. *Treasurer*—Wm. Suffern. *Secretary*—Dr. Kidley.[1]

---

(1). A well-known Medical Doctor at that time. In the year 1834 he was presented with a service of plate for his zeal and efficiency during the recent outbreak of Asiatic cholera in the town.

4th Feb., 1836. Resolved—That the Library in future shall be open Six days in the Week from 11 till 4 o'clock, and on the evenings of Monday, Tuesday, Wednesday, Thursday, and Friday from the hour of 6 till 8.

The time for opening was subsequently changed to 10 a.m., and in the evenings from 7 till 9, and it was resolved—

2nd June. That as long as the Library shall be open from 10 a.m. till 4 p.m., and in the evening from 7 till 9, the Librarian's salary shall be £45 per annum.

Mr. M'Ewen resigned his post as Librarian towards the close of the year.

The balance sheet showed—Receipts, £270 16s. 1d.; Expenditure, £177 0s. 8d. Number of Subscribers, 178.

1837.

President—Rev. Wm. Bruce. *Vice-President*—Wm. Thompson.[1] *Treasurer*—Wm. Suffern. *Secretary*—Dr. Kidley.

It being reported that several subscribers were desirous of having works of science in the Library, chiefly foreign, and having agreed to subscribe an additional guinea each for the purpose on certain conditions—

5th Jan. Agreed—That the principle be adopted, and that three members of the Committee be appointed to confer with three of the proposed Subscribers to settle the conditions. The six appear to have been—

Mr. Drummond Anderson	Mr. Wm. Thompson
Dr. M'Cluney	Mr. James M'Adam
Dr. Kidley	Dr. Thomas Andrews, F.R.S.[2]

On February 2nd, the following resolutions were adopted :—

2nd Feb. That the name of the "Belfast Society for Promoting Knowledge" be changed to that of "Belfast Library and Society for Promoting Knowledge."

That the Committee meet twice in the month in future—that is, on the first and third Thursday—instead of once in the month, as heretofore.

That should any member of the Library wish to have a restricted book at a time when it is not convenient to wait for the next meeting of Committee, the Librarian shall be empowered to lend not more than two vols. to such member, on his depositing the full value of the entire Work to which such vols. belong, as is marked in Librarian's List.

At the Committee meeting of August 4th—

4th Aug. Mr. Wm. Thompson reports having obtained Twenty-one Subscribers to the Scientific Fund of the Library on the terms agreed to at the Annual Meeting in February last, viz. :—That the Society subscribe an equal

---

(1). William Thompson, Esq., was one of the most distinguished of Irish Naturalists. He was author of the *Natural History of Ireland*, and from 1843 to 1852 was President of the Natural History and Philosophical Society.

(2). Professor of Chemistry, and first Vice-President, Queen's College, Belfast.

4th Aug., 1837. amount. Resolved—In conformity with the same, that the Treasurer be ordered to advance to Wm. Thompson, Treasurer to the Scientific Fund, the sum of £22 1s. od.

6th Oct. The Committee for the first time exercised the power recently conferred upon them by the Society of appointing the Librarian, and elected Mr. James Stewart to that office this day in place of Mr. M'Ewen.

A set of the *Belfast News-Letter* from the commencement having been offered by Mr. Henry Joy to be deposited in the Library, on condition that he should be at liberty to re-claim the same should he settle at any time in the North of Ireland, it was resolved—

7th Dec. That the above offer be accepted, and that the *News-Letter* be kept in the Library, and not allowed to be lent out without the joint permission of Mr. Joy and the Committee.

The balance sheet showed—Receipts, £292 6s. 10d.; Expenditure, £227 10s. 10d. Number of Subscribers, 177.

1838.

President—Rev. Wm. Bruce. *Vice-President*—Rev. Wm. Cairns.[1] *Treasurer*—W. T. Harvey.[2] *Secretary*—Dr. Kidley.

On the 1st February the following letter was ordered to be addressed to Mr. Joy :—

> DEAR SIR,—By order of the Committee of the Belfast Library, I return you their thanks for the copy of the *Belfast News-Letter* which has been deposited by your order in the Library. The Committee desire me further to say that they will take all possible care of your valuable loan, but that they cannot be responsible for the completeness of the Volumes at present, nor for any injury that may be sustained from Fire or otherwise. They have entered into the following Resolution for the greater security of the Books :—
>
> **7th Dec.** Resolved—That it (the *News-Letter*) be kept in the Library, and not lent out without the joint permission of Mr. Joy and the Committee.

19th April. Resolved—That temporary residents in Belfast or the neighbourhood may be permitted in the usual form to the use of the Library for one year on payment of Thirty Shillings Subscription ; the proposer becoming responsible for any loss which the Library may sustain.

Balance sheet showed—Receipts, £272 6s. 11d.; Expenditure, £283 4s. 11d.; paid Mr. W. Thompson towards Scientific Fund, included in above, £21 ; number of Subscribers, 179.

1839.

President—Rev. Wm. Bruce. *Vice-President*—Rev. Dr. Cairns. *Treasurer*—W. T. Harvey. *Secretary*—Dr. Kidley.

An Appendix to the Catalogue was ordered to be printed this year, but no copy of it is at present known to exist.

---

[1]. Professor of Logic, &c., Collegiate Department, Academical Institution.
[2]. Grain merchant and Insurance agent, Ritchie's Dock (now Corporation Square).

16th May, 1839.   A porter was engaged to call for and deliver Books "within the Lamps."

5th Sept.   Ordered—That the person who stole the Books and Librarian's cash be prosecuted.

The balance sheet showed—Receipts, £195 10s. ; Expenditure, £154 16s. 7d. ; to Mr. Thompson, for Scientific Fund, included in above, £21.   Number of Subscribers, 176.

1840.

President—Rev. Wm. Bruce.   *Vice-President*—Wm. Thompson.   *Treasurer*—W. T. Harvey.   *Secretary*—Dr. Kidley.

Committee—

Drummond Anderson	Rev. Dr. J. Seaton Reid	Jas. M'Adam
Dr. William M'Gee[1]	Rev. Dr. Cairns	Wm. Sinclair[5]
Rev. Dr. Bryce[2]	Rev. John Porter[3]	Wm. Bottomley[6]
Wm. Suffern	Wm. Webb[6]	

A statement having been prepared by Dr. J. S. Reid on the Use and Advantages of the Library, the same was ordered to be printed.

5th Mar.   Resolved—That temporary Residents, on depositing Two Guineas as a security for Books, be admitted to the Library at the usual Subscription of One Guinea per annum.

The balance sheet showed—Receipts, £245 3s. 5d. ; Expenditure, £252 5s. 1d. ; to Mr. Thompson, for Scientific Fund, included, £17 11s. 10d.   Number of Subscribers, 178.

1841.

President—Rev. Wm. Bruce.   *Vice-President*—Wm. Thompson.   *Treasurer*—W. T. Harvey.   *Secretary*—Dr. Kidley.

6th May.   A reward of £5 offered for the discovery of the person who injured *Wilson's Ornithology.*

The balance sheet showed—Receipts, £174 0s. 1d. ; Expenditure, £133 19s. 1d. ; to Mr. Thompson, for Scientific Fund, included, £15 9s. 6d.   Number of Subscribers, 165.

1842.

President—Rev. Wm. Bruce.   *Vice-President*—Wm. Thompson.   *Treasurer*—Wm. Bottomley.   *Secretary*—Dr. Kidley.

The year's proceedings were wholly routine.

The balance sheet showed—Receipts, £239 6s. 3d. ; Expenditure, £270 3s. 5d. ; to Mr. Wm. Thompson, for Scientific Fund, included, £14 14s.   Number of Subscribers, 189.

---

(1). Afterwards Vice-President and President of this Society.
(2). The Rev. R. J. Bryce, LL.D., Principal of the Belfast Academy, and Minister of the United Presbyterian Congregation, York Street ; also, author of several valuable books.
(3). Minister of the Second Presbyterian Church (Unitarian).
(4). Cotton yarn merchant, &c.
(5). Linen manufacturer and merchant.
(6). Wholesale warehouseman, Callender Street (Day & Bottomley).

1843.

President—Rev. Wm. Bruce. *Vice-President*—Wm. Thompson. *Treasurer*—Wm. Bottomley. *Secretary*—Dr. Kidley.

An important movement in the direction of admitting to membership on a wider basis than had hitherto obtained was made this year. On a recommendation by the Committee to reduce the entrance fee from two guineas to one guinea, it was resolved—

2nd Feb. That the recommendation of the Committee be agreed to with this understanding—That the new members who are admitted at the reduced entrance fee shall not have the power of transfer.

N.B.—Those admitted under this Resolution to be called "Members."

20th April. Resolved—That a new Catalogue, 8vo, be printed, agreeably to the plan of the Catalogue of the Dublin Society's Library—Doctors M'Gee and Burden[1] to have charge.

On 15th June the Earl of Enniskillen was elected an Honorary Member of the Society.

In November a deputation from the Law Society, consisting of Messrs. Garrett and Smith, waited on the Committee to propose terms for a junction with the Library. A sub-committee was appointed to confer; and on receiving their report it was resolved—

7th Dec. That this Committee cannot dispense with the usual entrance money received from the Subscribers.

In December a sub-committee was also appointed to wait upon the Committee of the Linen Hall to ask for additional space for the books.

The balance sheet showed—Receipts, £195 14s. 9d.; Expenditure, £232 3s. 8d.; for Scientific Fund, included in above, £24 12s. 3d. Number of Subscribers, 180.

1844.

President—Rev. Wm. Bruce. *Vice-President*—Wm. Thompson. *Treasurer*—Wm. Bottomley. *Secretary*—Dr. Kidley.

The negotiations with the Linen Hall Committee were reported in March in the following terms :—

7th Mar. Reported—That the Committee of the Linen Hall had consented to give for the use of the Library the two rooms [adjoining these], at present in occupation of the Linen Hall Committee, with the understanding that the Committees of the Linen Hall and Botanic Gardens should have the privilege of meeting in the Library.

The liberality of the Linen Hall Committee still further manifested itself during the year in connection with the following proposal, recorded 22nd June :—

22nd June. Resolved—That it is extremely desirable that the Committee room, Mr. Simms's room, the lobby, and the lumber room be thrown into one room, and the ceiling raised to the same height as the centre room, and that Mr. Thompson and Dr. M'Gee be requested to confer with the

(1). William Burden, Esq., M.D., Prof. Midwifery, Queen's College, and father of Henry Burden, Esq., M.D., a Member of Committee.

22nd June, 1844.
Committee of the Linen Hall to carry out the plan ; and that a copy of this resolution be signed by the Chairman, and transmitted to the Committee of the Linen Hall.

To this request the Committee acceded, on the understanding that the cost of alterations should be borne by the Society; and it was resolved—

3rd Jan., 1845.
That the thanks of the Belfast Library be returned to the Committee and Proprietors of the White Linen Hall for their liberality and public spirit in providing additional accommodation for the Library, by which it is now rendered, in a much greater degree, commensurate with the wants of this town and neighbourhood.

The arrangement with the Law Society, granting them the use of the Library under certain conditions, was also carried to a conclusion during the year. The heads of arrangement, five in number, were entered on the Minutes, and duly signed, 18th July.

It was also resolved on the same date—

18th July.
That the Curator to the Belfast Museum shall in future have access to this Library.

The additional cost of shelving the new rooms was partly raised by subscription, £28 being contributed during the following year by members.

The balance sheet showed—Receipts, £219 7s. (which included £32 11s. from the Law Society, according to agreement); Expenditure, £203 11s. 2½d.; amount paid towards Scientific Fund, £24 18s., included ; number of Subscribers not given.

1845.

President—Rev. Wm. Bruce. *Vice-President*—Wm. Thompson. *Treasurer*—Wm. Bottomley. *Secretary*—Dr. Kidley.

The business of the year was wholly routine.

The balance sheet showed—Receipts (including the amount subscribed for new shelves), £218 19s. 5d. ; Expenditure, £218 19s. 3½d., leaving a balance on the right side of 1½d. ; for Scientific Fund, included in above, £15 4s. 6d.

1846.

President—Rev. Wm. Bruce. *Vice-President*—Wm. Thompson. *Treasurer*—Wm. Bottomley. *Secretary*—Dr. Kidley.

Dr. Hincks, whose active interest in the Society during the five years he had already served as Vice-President, has frequently been noticed, made a valuable gift during this year of a Set of Valpy's Delphin Classics, in 157 volumes. The Society showed its appreciation of this generous donation—by no means the first it had received from Dr. Hincks—in the following resolution :—

21st May.
That in future the Rev. Dr. Hincks and his two daughters, and his son the Revd. Dr. Edward Hincks shall be Honorary Members of this Library, with the privilege of taking out Books.

The following Minutes relate to the recent regulation respecting strangers :—

15th Oct., 1846. That the Rule for admitting strangers to the Library does not apply to Students coming in from the country for half a year.

That the admission of Students has been found to interfere with the rights and convenience of Subscribers to such an extent that it is now necessary it should be refused.

That copies of these resolutions be sent to the Professors at the Royal Academical Institution, and be posted on the door.

The balance sheet showed—Receipts, £195 18s. 6½d.; Expenditure, £206 11s. 7d.; for Scientific Fund, included in above, £17 17s.

1847.

President—Rev. Wm. Bruce. *Vice-President*—Wm. Thompson. *Treasurer*—Wm. Bottomley. *Secretary*—Dr. Kidley.

Routine business only was transacted.

The balance sheet showed—Receipts, £191 19s. 6d. ; Expenditure, £198 9s. 1½d.; for Scientific Fund, included in above, £15 15s.

1848.

President—Rev. Wm. Bruce. *Vice-President*—Wm. Thompson. *Treasurer*—Wm. Bottomley. *Secretary*—Dr. Kidley.

Routine business only transacted.

The balance sheet showed—Receipts, £192 12s. 7d. ; Expenditure, £193 16s. 3d. ; for Scientific Fund, included in above, £11 11s.

1849.

President—Rev. Wm. Bruce. *Vice-President*—Wm. Thompson. *Treasurer*—Wm. Bottomley. *Secretary*—Dr. Kidley.

The Library was ordered to be kept closed on the evenings of Tuesday, Thursday, and Saturday during the summer months.

2nd Aug. No books to be entered in the proposal book but by actual Subscribers.

6th Oct. Application to be made to the local Corporate Bodies for copies of their Acts of Parliament relating to the town.

The balance sheet showed—Receipts, £210 2s. 10d. ; Expenditure, £172 10s. 1d. ; for Scientific Fund, included in above, £10 10s.

1850.[1]

President—Rev. Wm. Bruce. *Vice-President*—Wm. Thompson. *Treasurer*—Wm. Bottomley. *Secretary*—Dr. Kidley.

Committee—

Jas. M'Adam	Dr. Drennan	Wm. Simms
Dr. Hodges	Wm. Ferguson	Dr. Bryce
Dr. M'Gee	Wm. Suffern	Thos. Chermside
Geo. K. Smith	Dr. Andrews	

(1). Personal Notes are discontinued after this date, many Members being still alive.

7th Feb., 1850.   Ordered—That no child whatever be admitted into the large room, and that none but Subscribers be allowed to take books from the shelves.

In April an arrangement was come to with the President and Professors at Queen's College, Belfast, as follows :—

4th April.   1. That the President and Professors of Queen's College be admitted to consult any Books in this Library.

2. That, with a written order from any of the above persons, students may be admitted if engaged in the study of any particular subject, but only two at a time.

3. That the President and Members of Committee of the Belfast Library be admitted to the Queen's College Library.

4. That the other members of the White Linen Hall be admitted to Queen's College Library on producing a line from any office-bearer of that Library.

Application was ordered to be made to the Academical Institution for the Maps of the Ordnance Survey lodged there.

Those valuable maps, on the 6-inch scale, of the whole series for Ireland, were afterwards deposited in the Library, a special case being prepared to contain them.

The balance sheet is not given.

1851.

President—Rev. Wm. Bruce.   *Vice-President*—Wm. Thompson.   *Treasurer*—Wm. Bottomley.   *Secretary*—Dr. Kidley.

A new Catalogue was ordered, and was printed by R. & D. Read at their contract price, £19 1s. 6d.

The balance sheet is again omitted.

1852.

President—Rev. Wm. Bruce.   *Vice-President*—Wm. Thompson.   *Treasurer*—Wm. Bottomley.   *Secretary*—Dr. Kidley.

It was resolved, in February, to increase the insurance of the Library by £800.

Tenders were again invited from Belfast booksellers for supplying the Society with books and periodicals required; and Henry Greer, having offered to allow 15 per cent. from published prices, was chosen to supply the Library for one year.

The Society experienced a serious loss in the death of its worthy Vice-President, and passed the following resolution :—

18th Mar.   That we desire to record our deep regret at the death of our late Vice-President, William Thompson, Esq.; our strong sense of the value of his services, not merely to this Institution, but to the cause of Literature and Science; and we heartily sympathise with the affliction of his bereaved relatives.

On 6th May of this year Mr. Robert Gray was requested to act as Secretary in the place of Dr. Kidley.

The balance sheet of this year showed—Receipts, £208 1s. 6d.; Expenditure, £188 19s. 9d.

1853.

President—Rev. Wm. Bruce. *Vice-President*—Dr. Wm. M'Gee. *Treasurer*—Wm. Bottomley. *Secretary*—Robert Gray.

3rd Feb.   Resolved—That any officer of the Belfast Garrison, on being introduced by the Commanding Officer of the Regiment, be admitted to read in the Library during his stay in town on entering his name in a book to be kept for that purpose, and that a copy of this Resolution be transmitted to the Commanding Officer.

5th May.   Resolved—That Petitions be sent to Parliament, through our member, Mr. Richard Davison, and to Lord Dufferin, for copies of the Reports presented to the House.

The balance sheet showed— Receipts, £220 12s. 7d.; Expenditure, £212 4s. 6d.

1854.

President—Rev. Wm. Bruce. *Vice-President*—Dr. M'Gee. *Treasurer*—William Bottomley. *Secretary*—Robert Gray.

Routine work only was transacted.

The balance sheet showed—Receipts, £216 12s. 11d.; Expenditure, £200 12s.

1855.

President—Rev. Wm. Bruce. *Vice-President*—Dr. M'Gee. *Treasurer*—William Bottomley. *Secretary*—Robert Gray.

An Appendix to the Catalogue was printed during the year.

The balance sheet showed—Receipts, £212 9s. 11d.; Expenditure, £223 19s. 7d.

1856.

President—Rev. Wm. Bruce. *Vice-President*—Dr. M'Gee. *Treasurer*—William Bottomley. *Secretary*—Robert Gray.

Routine business only was transacted.

The balance sheet showed—Receipts, £239 16s. 6d.; Expenditure, £244 2s. 9d.

1857.

President—Rev. Wm. Bruce. *Vice-President*—Dr. M'Gee. *Treasurer*—William Bottomley. *Secretary*—Robert Gray.

The question of admitting certain members without entrance fee once more came to the front, and the following important resolutions were come to :—

10th Jan.   That for the year ending 31st December, 1857, Subscribers, on being balloted for, shall be admissible by paying *One Guinea*, without entrance fee ; such Subscribers to have the use of the Library (to the same extent as members), with power to propose books, but no other privilege.

That the Committee shall have the power of withdrawing or suspending any or all these privileges from any individual on finding that they have been abused by him.

5th Feb.   That persons in the employment of Proprietors· or Members may become Subscribers on receiving a guarantee from their employers, and on

5th Feb., 1857. being balloted for and paying *Half a Guinea* per annum ; such persons to . have permission to read in the Library, and take out one volume at a time, but to possess no other privilege, and to be subject to such other regulations as the Committee shall from time to time enact.

Thus, after long hesitation and many heart-burnings, this vexed question was brought to a satisfactory settlement, and the basis of the Society was broadened to adapt it to the circumstances of almost all for whose benefit it was established.

A proposition to appoint the President, Vice-President, and Treasurer as Trustees for the Library property was deferred.

It was also resolved—

5th Feb.　　　That henceforth any Proprietor or Member who may be desirous of perusing at his own residence any printed book, the circulation of which has been singly restricted by the Committee, shall have the power of procuring the same by order from any Member of the Committee on depositing in the Librarian's hands the full value of the work, if required, and giving him a written acknowledgment for the book.

That any person wishing to become a Subscriber, if balloted for and approved of, shall be admitted at any period of the year on paying one year's subscription, together with any part of the current year still unexpired.

The balance sheet is omitted.

1858.

President—Rev. Wm. Bruce. *Vice-President*—Dr. M'Gee. *Treasurer*—William Bottomley. *Secretary*—Robert Gray.

John Graham was appointed Assistant Librarian.

The balance sheet is omitted.

1859.

President—Rev. Wm. Bruce. *Vice-President*—Dr. M'Gee. *Treasurer*—William Bottomley. *Secretary*—Robert Gray.

In relation to the recent decision to admit apprentices as readers at a reduced subscription, it was agreed—

20th Jan.　　　That in future any Proprietor or Member of the Library be competent to be a guarantee of half-guinea subscribers, whether the latter be in his employment or not.

The balance sheet is omitted.

1860.

President—Rev. Wm. Bruce. *Vice-President*—Dr. M'Gee. *Treasurer*—William Bottomley. *Secretary*—Robert Gray.

Committee—

Dr. Bryce	James M'Adam	Wm. Browne
Dr. Drennan	Joseph J. Murphy	Wm. M'Ilwrath
Rev. James Young	Wm. Simms	Robert Young
Dr. Hodges	A. C. Weir	

2nd Feb., 1860. Resolved—That the Rev. W. Bruce, Rev. James Young, and Mr. Bottomley be appointed a sub-committee to draw up a circular stating the advantages to be derived from being members or readers in the Linen Hall Library, and that said circular be printed and placed in merchants' offices.

A copy of the circular is entered on the Minutes on May 15th.

The balance sheet showed—Receipts, £323 19s. 6d. (including £4 7s. 6d. for books sold to Queen's College, Belfast); Expenditure, £255 14s.

1861.

President—Rev. William Bruce. *Vice-President*—Dr. M'Gee. *Treasurer*—William Bottomley. *Secretary*—Robert Gray.

The death of an old supporter of the Society is noted as follows :—

15th May. Resolved—That the Committee desire, on the occasion of their first meeting after the decease of Mr. James M'Adam, so long a valuable member of our body, to give expression to the deep regard and sincere respect which they entertained for him personally, to the high appreciation in which they held his Literary and Scientific acquirements, and the regret which the announcement of his death elicited; and, further, that our chairman, Dr. M'Gee, be requested to convey to his relatives the expression of our condolence on the bereavement which they have sustained.

On August 1st, Dr. Bryce and Mr. J. J. Murphy were nominated to attend the meeting of the National Association for Promotion of Social Science on the 14th instant.

17th Oct. Ordered—That Dr. W. B. Ritchie be allowed out the Ordnance Maps of County Donegal, 110 sheets, on his depositing £10 with the Librarian.

A new Catalogue was printed this year by Mr. Alexander Mayne, under the direction of the President. This Catalogue was sold at one shilling each (500 copies issued).

Balance sheet omitted.

1862.

President—Rev. William Bruce. *Vice-President*—Dr. M'Gee. *Treasurer*—William Bottomley. *Secretary*—Robert Gray.

2nd Oct. It was resolved that the Committee be authorised to make arrangements with the London Library Company, Limited, for a supply and return of books.

Owing to a difference of opinion regarding the management of the Society's affairs, a Sub-Committee was appointed to inquire into the general state of the Library, and report thereon. This they did on 16th October. The report states that they find, during the past five years, a gradual decrease in the number of Subscribers, until, in the present year, there is a falling-off of thirty-one guinea Subscribers and twenty-six half-guinea, causing a decrease of £45 3s. in the funds of the Library. The Sub-Committee proceed to set forth the causes for the decline, the chief of them being—

F

6th Oct., 1862.   1. The difficulty of obtaining new books.

2. The want of that class of books most in request (*i.e.*, the light literature of the day).

3. The terms of admission.

4. The advantages possessed by the Library not being sufficiently known to the public.

These points were left for the consideration of the Society.

The balance sheet showed—Receipts, £219 11s. 7d. ; Expenditure, £220 1s. 3d.

1863.

President—Rev. William Bruce.   *Vice-President*—Dr. M'Gee.   *Treasurer*—William Bottomley.   *Secretary*—Robert Gray.

The unfavourable report of the Sub-Committee in the preceding year appears to have suggested a pretty thorough reorganisation of the affairs of the Society, and the following Minutes indicate the directions in which it was hoped the reform might be effected :—

5th Feb.   Ordered—That the Committee have a statement of accounts published and sent out to each Shareholder or Proprietor one week before the Annual Meeting.

That the Committee be empowered to connect this Library for one year with the London Library Company, Limited, under such restrictions as they may find judicious.

5th Feb.   Notice of motion for an adjourned meeting in March was given by Dr. Ritchie—That the Committee shall consist of twelve members, and that three retire in rotation and be not eligible for re-election for one year.

Notice of motion by the Rev. J. Scott Porter—That the Rule admitting Members and Subscribers without the full admission fee of Two Guineas be rescinded, reserving to existing Members and Subscribers any rights which they may have already acquired.

The two orders as above were acted upon ; and £7 15s. was allotted for the purpose of obtaining 30 volumes of books from the London Library Company, Ltd., under the direction of a Sub-Committee. The two notices of motion, however, as well as a third, which also threatened to disturb the arrangement which had been come to in reference to the enlargement of the membership of the Society, were defeated, as will appear by the following Minutes :—

At an Adjourned Meeting of Shareholders and Members, held March 19th—

19th Mar.   I. Dr. Ritchie's motion was rejected.

II. Proposed by Robert Patterson, and seconded by Stephen Archer —That the two classes of Members, those paying an entrance fee of One Guinea and those paying an entrance fee of Two Guineas, be continued as heretofore, and that the admission of new Annual Subscribers at the rate of One Guinea, without an entrance fee, be discontinued at the end of the present year, and that half-guinea Subscribers be continued under the same regulations as at present.

19th Mar., 1863.   This proposal was lost by a majority of one.

III. Proposed by the Rev. John Scott Porter, seconded by Dr. W. M'Gee—That those portions of the existing laws which sanction the admission of Members paying an admission fee of One Guinea, and of Guinea Subscribers not paying any admission fee, be and the same are hereby rescinded. Provided always, that persons who have already been admitted as Members, or as Guinea Subscribers under the regulations which are hereby rescinded, shall possess and enjoy all the privileges to which they are now entitled so long as their respective subscriptions shall continue to be paid.

Lost by the casting vote of the Chairman.

Here it will be observed that two attempts made to diminish the usefulness of this Library were defeated —one by a very narrow majority, and the other by the casting vote of the President.

Had the President voted on the other side the consequence would have been that in a very short time, instead of the flourishing Society of to-day, numbering 836 Subscribers, it would have dwindled down to 64 Proprietors, a number considerably less than that first recorded.

The memory of the late Rev. Wm. Bruce should therefore be regarded with the greatest respect and esteem as that of one who saved this Library from such an unenviable fate.

5th Mar.   Resolved unanimously—That the engraving of the late Dr. Bruce, presented to the Library by Dr. M'Gee, be accepted, and hung up in the Western Room. He was a Member for twenty-five years, and for nineteen years President of the Society for Promoting Knowledge.

The balance sheet showed—Receipts, £225 9s. 8d.; Expenditure, £226 9s. 4d. (including £7 7s. 3d. for books on loan from the London Library Company, Limited).

1864.

President—Rev. William Bruce.   *Vice-President*—Dr. M'Gee.   *Treasurer*—William Bottomley.   *Secretary*—Robert Gray.

The amount set aside for procuring books on loan from the London Library Co., Ltd., this year was £15.

The question of the subscription fees was again raised, and resulted in the following compromise :—

15th Feb.   Adjourned meeting—Moved by Dr. M'Gee, seconded by Dr. Bryce, and resolved—That, to annual Subscribers hereafter to be admitted, the subscription shall be twenty-five shillings instead of one guinea as heretofore.

To this an amendment was proposed by the Rev. Dr. M'Ilwaine and seconded by the Rev. James Young—

That it is inexpedient to raise the rate of subscription for Annual Subscribers, and that it shall continue at the present sum of One Guinea ; but that in future the privilege of such Annual Subscribers be limited to reading in the Library, and being permitted to borrow two vols. at a time.

The amendment was adopted.

The balance sheet showed—Receipts, £222 11s. 11d. ; Expenditure, £206 6s. 6d.

1865.

President—Rev. William Bruce.   *Vice-President*—Dr. M'Gee.   *Treasurer*—William Bottomley.   *Secretary*—Robert Gray.

As on the present occasion a large proportion of new members were elected on the Committee, we subjoin the list :—

Committee—

Rev. Jas. Young	Rev. W. M'Ilwaine	Rev. W. C. M'Cullagh
A. C. Weir	John Workman	Dr. Samuel Browne, R.N.
Henry Reid	John Anderson	Rev. Robt. Workman
J. J. Murphy	Robert Young.	

2nd Feb.   Resolved—That there be a thorough revision of the laws, for the purpose of making such additions, retrenchments, and alterations consistent with the fundamental constitution of the Society as existing circumstances may to them appear expedient.

This task occupied a considerable time, and when completed, 300 copies of the new Laws were ordered to be printed and circulated.—*(See Appendix.)*

The arrangement with the London Library Co., Ltd., appears to have given place to a similar arrangement with Mudie's Library, to which a subscription of £14 14s. for the current year, was paid for the loan of such books as should be selected by a Sub-Committee.

The venerable rule of the Society excluding fiction and books of trivial amusement was found at last to require some modification, and a cautious beginning was thus made in the direction of supplying a class of literature which had attractions for a considerable number of the Subscribers.

On December 6th Dr. James Moore, having presented the Society with eight parts of the Transactions of the Royal Irish Academy, and offering to continue to send further publications of the same body, was elected an Honorary Member.

The balance sheet of this year gave an encouraging proof of the fresh vigour which had been infused into the Society by recent changes, and showed—Receipts, £305 11s. 4d.; Expenditure, £244 13s. 0d. (including £16 4s. 5d. for books on loan from Mudie's, London).

1866.

President—Rev. William Bruce.   *Vice-President*—Dr. M'Gee.   *Treasurer*—William Bottomley.   *Secretary*—Robert Gray.

At the first meeting of the year a report was presented showing a balance in hand of £66 13s. 9d., "a considerable portion of which consists of entrance fees paid by annual subscribers on becoming Proprietors and Members." It was thereupon resolved—

15th Feb., 1866. That the amount to be applied to the procuring of books on loan from Mudie's or other party be left to the discretion of the Committee for the time being, but not in any case to exceed £50.

The amount actually subscribed to Mudie's under this resolution was £45 2s. 4d.

The balance sheet showed—Receipts, £383 10s. 2d. ; Expenditure, £338 12s. 6d.

1867.

President—Rev. William Bruce. *Vice-President*—Dr. M'Gee. *Treasurer*—William Bottomley. *Secretary*—Robert Gray.

The business transacted was wholly routine.

The balance sheet showed—Receipts, £373 13s. 3d. ; Expenditure, £339 1s. 8d. (including £58 paid to Mudie's).

1868.

President—Rev. William Bruce. *Vice-President*—Dr. M'Gee. *Treasurer*—William Bottomley. *Secretary*—Robert Gray.

The Society was deprived this year of its Librarian, Mr. Stewart, who for thirty-one years had filled the post ; and the following resolution was placed on the Minutes :—

6th Aug. Resolved—That the Committee have heard with much regret of the death of Mr. James Stewart, who for a period of thirty-one years filled the responsible office of Librarian to this Society ; and that they now feel it to be their melancholy duty to place on record this memorial of his long and faithful services, and of their high esteem for him as an upright and honourable man.

At the same meeting Mr. James Stephens, who had acted for six years as Sub-Librarian, was appointed Librarian.

A still more heavy loss befell the Society in the death of its honoured and worthy President, the Rev. William Bruce, who for fifty-two years had devoted unceasing time, attention, and judgment to the interests of the members. The following resolution was passed on 5th November :—

5th Nov. Resolved—That the Committee of the Belfast Society for the Promotion of Knowledge feel called upon to express to the family of the late Revd. Wm. Bruce, their President, their high estimate of the valuable services rendered by him to this Society during a very lengthened period, and their deep sympathy with them under their late heavy bereavement.

The balance sheet showed—Receipts, £355 17s. 11d. ; Expenditure, £288 7s. 1d. (including £57 18s. 8d. paid to Mudie's).

1869.

President—Dr. Wm. M'Gee. *Vice-President*—Joseph John Murphy. *Treasurer*—Wm. Bottomley. *Secretary*—Robert Gray.

The following letter was received from Mr. W. B. Joy, of Dublin, in October, and entered on the Minutes :—

21st Oct., 1869.   London, *October 21st,* 1869.

    Sir,—In my house in Dublin, which I am on the point of giving up, I have a large
full-length portrait of the late Dr. Bruce, who took a great interest in his day in the
formation of your Library, as did his son, the late Rev. Wm. Bruce, in its subsequent
management. If it were acceptable to your Committee, I should be happy to present it
to the Library if you have any suitable place for hanging it. I would have it forwarded
to them free of all expense. An early reply—if possible by the beginning of next week,
as I have to give up my house immediately—would much oblige,

Yours, dear Sir, truly,

Wm. B. Joy.

The Librarian, Belfast Library,

    Linen Hall, Donegall Square.

    This generous offer was suitably responded to by the President in the name of the
Society; and this portrait (which, however, is not correctly described as full length) now
adorns the Western Room.

    The balance sheet showed—Receipts, £377 10s. 4d.; Expenditure, £341 0s. 5d.
(including £57 15s. subscribed to Mudie's for " works of light and popular literature.")

1870.

    President—Dr. M'Gee.   *Vice-President*—J. J. Murphy.   *Treasurer*—Wm. Bottomley.
Secretary—Robert Gray.

Committee—

Rev. Dr. Porter	John Workman	Wm. Simms
W. F. Crothers	Wm. Browne	A. C. Weir
John Anderson	Rev. W. C. M'Cullagh	John Corry
Henry Reid	W. D. Henderson	

    The report presented at the commencement of this year mentions the gratifying fact,
that more books had been added during the past year to the Library than in any one
during the last fifteen years, the total number of volumes now amounting to 16,000; also,
that the number of books in circulation during the year had greatly exceeded those of
any former year.

    The Insurance on the Library was increased to £4,000.

    The following interesting correspondence speaks for itself :—

8th Jan.   Linen Hall Library, *8th January,* 1870.

    Sir,—The Committee of the Linen Hall Library beg leave to offer to your Com-
mittee the accompanying engraved portrait of the late Dr. Bruce, in the hope that it may
be placed in your Committee room, or some other room in your building.

    Dr. Bruce long took very much interest in your Institution, and was for many years
a zealous and watchful member of its Committee.

Yours respectfully,

W. M'Gee, *President.*

To the Chairman and Committee of the

    Belfast Charitable Society.

11th Jan., 1870.
BELFAST CHARITABLE SOCIETY, 11th Jan., 1870.

SIR,—The Committee of the above Society have received your letter of the 8th inst., with the accompanying portrait of the late Dr. Bruce, which has been so handsomely presented.

Resolved—That the thanks of the Committee of the Belfast Charitable Society be given to the Committee of the Linen Hall Library for the gift of the portrait of the late Dr. Bruce, and that it will be hung in the Board-room.

EDWD. DESPARD, *Hon. Sec.*

A new Catalogue was ordered to be prepared under the superintendence of Messrs. Murphy, Anderson, MacAdam, and the Rev. Dr. Porter.

The balance sheet showed—Receipts, £364 8s. 11d.; Expenditure, £319 15s. 11d. (including £73 10s. 0d. to Mudie's).

1871.

President—Dr. M'Gee. *Vice-President*—J. J. Murphy. *Treasurer*—Wm. Bottomley. *Secretary*—Robert Gray.

The amount placed this year at the disposal of the Committee for procuring books from Mudie's was £85.

The following Minutes are interesting as pointing to the first steps taken by the Committee in the direction of a local Bibliography, an undertaking which during the past few months has been brought to a successful termination :—

16th Feb. Resolved—That the Committee do consider the propriety of making a small collection of early-printed books, especially those printed in Ireland, and more particularly in Belfast.

6th April. That a circular approved by the Committee be sent out, requesting aid in the formation of a collection of Books printed in Belfast.

20th May. Resolved—That the tender of the *News-Letter* be accepted for printing the new Catalogue, and that Messrs. John Anderson and Robert MacAdam correct same for the press, and see it through, and that 750 copies be struck off.

The Librarian, Mr. Joseph Stephens, tendered his resignation in September, which was accepted ; and the Assistant Librarian, Mr. Joseph Watson, was appointed his successor.

Permission was given to Subscribers to take out periodicals from closing hour at night to opening time the next morning.

The balance sheet showed—Receipts, £360 1s. 11d. ; Expenditure, £338 17s. 0d. (including £84 1s. 0d. to Mudie's).

1872.

President—Dr. M'Gee. *Vice-President*—J. J. Murphy. *Treasurer*—Wm. Bottomley. *Secretary*—Robert Gray.

Mr. Gray, early in the year, gave notice of his intention to resign, after nearly twenty years' service. The Society received the announcement with regret, and voted their thanks to Mr. Gray for his valuable services. Until the appointment of a successor, Mr. William Browne undertook the duty.

15th Feb., 1872.   Thanks of the Society voted to Messrs. Robert MacAdam and John Anderson for their valuable aid in the preparation of the MS. Catalogue, and in the subsequent revision of the proof sheets.

The last appointment to the Librarian's office not proving satisfactory, a further change was made, resulting in the appointment of Mr. Francis A. Maitland to the post on October 17th.

In December an arrangement was entered into with the Proprietors of the Linen Hall for the use of the large room adjoining the Library to the east, known as the News-room, which is to be added to the Library; and Messrs. Simms, Anderson, and MacAdam were appointed a Sub-Committee to make the necessary alterations.

On the motion of Mr. W. E. Crothers, the following six Sub-Committees were appointed in December for the better working of the Library :—1, Repairs; 2, Librarian's Duties; 3, Mudie's; 4, Finance; 5, Classification; 6, Purchase.

The balance sheet showed—Receipts, £401 18s. 4d.; Expenditure, £369 12s. 3d. (including £84 1s. 0d. to Mudie's).

1873.

President—Dr. M'Gee.   *Vice-President*—J. J. Murphy.   *Treasurer*—Wm. Bottomley. *Secretary*—John Anderson.

On February 20th, the sum of £85 was voted

20th Feb.   For procuring works of light literature or of fiction, and that in expending this amount, the Committee are hereby empowered to purchase works of this class, where they may find it cheaper to do so than to obtain them on loan.

The amount to be spent in the purchase of novels was at a subsequent meeting fixed at £35, and at the same time it was agreed to discontinue the subscription to Mudie's.

A Proposal Book for the purchase of light literature was ordered to be kept.

It was resolved to appropriate the new room as a Reading Room.

It was also agreed that books should in future be purchased from W. H. Smith & Son instead of from Mr. Henry Greer; and further, it was ordered that the *Times* newspaper be taken in.

A Sub-Committee having reported in favour of a subject classification of the books, it was resolved—

25th June.   1st. That the entire Books of the Library be classified and shelved under fifteen compartments, viz :—

A. Theology and Biblical Literature	H. Political and Social Economy
B. Logic and Metaphysics	J. Fine and Industrial Arts
C. Science	K. Poetry and the Drama
D. Biography	L. Fiction
E. History	M. Classics and Philology
F. Geography and Travels	N. Miscellaneous
G. Law	O. Books of Reference
	P. Periodicals (Bound)

The details of this important re-arrangement were left to the Sub-Committee, who were empowered to act with the authority of the Committee.

In November the Library received a legacy of £10, bequeathed by the Rev. Wm. Breakey, of Lisburn, who died on the 6th April, 1872.

The balance sheet showed—Receipts, £445s 10s. 3d. ; Expenditure, £438 13s. 6d. (included £113 on account of the new room).

1874.

President—J. J. Murphy.   *Vice-President*—A. C. Weir.   *Treasurer*—Wm. Bottomley.
Secretary—John Anderson.

The death of Dr. M'Gee was felt to be a serious loss to the Society, who placed on record their appreciation of his services as follows :—

19th Feb. Resolved—That this meeting hereby expresses its sense of the great loss the Society has sustained by the death of the President, the late Dr. William M'Gee. Having been a member of the Society for nearly forty years, and having been successively a Member of Committee, Vice-President, and President, he was thoroughly conversant with its operations, and, by the warm interest that he took in its affairs, contributed largely to its present prosperity. The regularity and punctuality of his attendance, the wisdom of his counsels, the impartiality and dignity with which he discharged the duties of the chair, were often the subject of general observation ; and now that he is gone, the Members of the Society would record the obligations under which they have been placed by the variety and value of the services he so long and so cheerfully rendered.

19th Mar. Letter read from Robt. Joy, Esq., Craigavad, presenting the Library with a copy of *Horæ Otiosæ*, written by his father, and referring to the loan of the *Belfast News-Letter*. Ordered—That the Secretary thank Mr. Joy for his gift ; also, for the favour conferred on the Library by the loan of the valued copy of the *News-Letter* referred to.

Counsel's opinion was taken during the year as to the propriety of appointing Trustees of the Society's property, and being held to be adverse to the proposal, the matter was allowed to drop.

2nd April. Resolved—That in consideration of the long and honourable connection of Mr. Henry Greer with the Library, he be in future admitted to the privilege of an Annual Subscriber.

18th June. Ordered—That the Executive Committee appointed to make arrangements for the meeting of the British Association in Belfast, in August next, be informed that the Belfast Library will be open free to the members of the Association during their stay in Belfast.

15th Oct. The question of lending out the *News-Letter* having been considered, Resolved unanimously—That the Committee decline to entertain any application for its loan.

The balance sheet showed—Receipts, £457 18s. 5d.; Expenditure, £451 3s. 4d.

1875.

President—J. J. Murphy.   *Vice-President*—A. C. Weir.   *Treasurer*—Jas. T. Bristow.
Secretary—John Anderson.

The Society was called upon to lament a double loss this year—one in the death of its late Secretary, Mr. Robert Gray; the other in the retirement of its Treasurer. The following resolutions stand on the Minutes :—

18th Feb.   The death of Mr. Robert Gray since last meeting of Committee having been mentioned, the following resolution was passed unanimously :—

That the Committee enter on their Minutes their sincere regret at the death of Mr. Robert Gray, who was for many years connected with the Library as its Secretary and a Member of Committee, and who in both capacities zealously promoted its objects and the interests of the Shareholders, Members, and Subscribers.

The foregoing resolution to be signed by the President and Secretary, and communicated to Mrs. Gray.

Mr. Bottomley having resigned his office of Treasurer, Resolved—That the best thanks of the meeting are due, and are hereby tendered, to Mr. Wm. Bottomley for his long and faithful services as Hon. Treasurer.

The following resolutions relating to the extension of privileges to apprentices and young persons in the use of the Library were passed at a special meeting in November :—

18th Nov.   Meeting—That the following be substituted for Law 8 :—That apprentices and other young persons under twenty-one years of age, on a satisfactory guarantee, shall be eligible for admission to the Library on payment of half a guinea per annum, and shall have the right to take out one book and to read in the Library, but without further privilege. This privilege will require renewal annually.

The Committee shall also have power to admit other persons, under special circumstances, to the same privilege, on the same conditions as to payment, guarantee, and renewal. All 10/6 Subscribers are eligible to become 21/- Subscribers without a new Ballot.

The balance sheet showed—Receipts, £458 3s. 6d.; Expenditure, £437 12s. 1d. (including Novels purchased, £26 7s. 6d.).

1876.

President—J. J. Murphy.   *Vice-President*—A. C. Weir.   *Treasurer*—Jas. T. Bristow.
Secretary—John Anderson.

The Report for this year gives the following account of the state of the Library :—

As the Library at present contains upwards of 17,000 vols., many of which are valuable as works of reference, and as the lighter literature of the day is well represented, and includes the more prominent Reviews and Illustrated Papers, and as the accommodation is now ample and con-

1876. venient, it is desirable that a much greater number of the inhabitants of the town and neighbourhood should seek admission during the current year.

It was agreed, on a recommendation of the Committee, to increase the amount allowed for the purchase of Novels, &c., to £50.

The total sum for which the property of the Society was insured this year was £6,000.

The balance sheet showed—Receipts, £489 1s. 4d. ; Expenditure, £461 19s. 3d. (including Novels, £34 7s. 1d.).

1877.

President—J. J. Murphy. *Vice-President*—A. C. Weir. *Treasurer*—Jas. T. Bristow. *Secretary*—John Anderson.

The business of the year was almost wholly routine.

The balance sheet showed—Receipts, £515 16s. 5d. ; Expenditure, £498 4s. 2d. (including Novels, £40 2s. 3d.).

1878.

President—J. J. Murphy. *Vice-President*—A. C. Weir. *Treasurer*—Thomas Montgomery. *Secretary*—John Anderson.

A revision of the Library took place during the year. It was reported that a certain number of volumes, of which a list was presented, were missing.

Mr. George Benn, the venerable historian of Belfast, being engaged, despite his failing eyesight, in collecting materials for the continuation of his history, made application to be allowed to have out the *Belfast News-Letter*, a volume at a time, as he may require it. It was thereupon resolved—

3rd Oct. That Mr. Benn's request, under the circumstances, may be complied with, his case being an exceptional one.[1]

The balance sheet showed—Receipts, £515 17s. 3d. ; Expenditure, £492 3s. 1d. (including Novels, £22 15s. 7d.)

1879.

President—J. J. Murphy. *Vice-President*—A. C. Weir. *Treasurer*—Thomas Montgomery. *Secretary*—John Anderson.

In April the Committee subscribed for a copy of the Minutes of the General Synod of Ulster, 1691-1820, edited by Dr. Killen and Rev. J. H. Orr, now being prepared for publication.

4th Dec. Mr. W. Edmund Crothers having resigned his seat at the Board, the Committee resolved—That they desire to place upon record their high appreciation of his valuable services, and the great interest which he invariably took in the management of the Society's affairs, during the long period of fourteen years, in which he uninterruptedly sat as a Member.

---

[1]. Mr. Benn's Continuation (Vol. II.), here referred to, owing to his infirmity, was only partially accomplished. His *History of the Town of Belfast from the Earliest Times to the Close of the Eighteenth Century*, with maps and illustrations, Vol. I., 8vo, was published by Marcus Ward & Co., London and Belfast, in 1877, and contains much interesting information concerning the town and its inhabitants.

A Supplement to the Catalogue was ordered.

The balance sheet showed—Receipts, £557 10s. od.; Expenditure, £539 7s. 9d. (including Novels, £29 11s. 9d.)

1880.

President—J. J. Murphy.   *Vice-President*—A. C. Weir.   *Treasurer*—Thomas Montgomery.   *Secretary*—John Anderson.

Committee—

Dr. Drennan	R. MacGeagh	W. A. Robinson
Dr. Hodges	Rev. W. C. M'Cullagh	W. Simms
W. D. Henderson	W. H. Patterson	John Workman
R. MacAdam	H. Reid	

A new 5-inch Rain Gauge was ordered to be purchased in January.

The balance sheet showed—Receipts, £578 14s. 9d.; Expenditure, £561 2s. 11d. (including Novels, £38 3s. 6d.)

1881.

President—J. J. Murphy.   *Vice-President*—A. C. Weir.   *Treasurer*—Thomas Montgomery.   *Secretary*—John Anderson.

In February it was agreed that Mr. Samuel A. Stewart, Scientific Curator of the Belfast Museum, should be admitted free to the Library.

The business of the year was wholly routine.

The balance sheet showed—Receipts, £608 19s. 9d.; Expenditure, £592 4s. 10d. (including Novels, £36 17s. od.).

1882.

President—J. J. Murphy.   *Vice-President*—A. C. Weir.   *Treasurer*—Thomas Montgomery.   *Secretary*—John Anderson.

A new Catalogue was ordered to be prepared, under the direction of Messrs. R. MacAdam, J. Anderson, and J. Wilson.

In view of the large increase of the Library, and the consequent tax upon the shelf space, Dr. Drennan and Mr. Robert Young were appointed to withdraw useless works from the shelves and Catalogue.

The balance sheet showed—Receipts, £617 15s. 1d.; Expenditure, £596 13s. od. The sum expended on Novels during the year was only £20 11s. 10d.

1883.

President—J. J. Murphy.   *Vice-President*—A. C. Weir.   *Treasurer*—Thomas Montgomery.   *Secretary*—John Anderson.

Early in the year the death of the Vice-President, Mr. A. C. Weir, occurred, and the following resolution on the event was recorded :—

1st Mar.   Resolved—That at this the first meeting of the Society since the death of our respected Vice-President, A. C. Weir, we desire to express our great regret at that event, and the loss the Library has sustained by the death of one of its most respected and useful members. During the many

1st Mar., 1883. years Mr. Weir filled the offices of Member of Committee and Vice-President, we found in him a most efficient assistant in conducting its affairs, and a most courteous colleague.

On 5th April Dr. J. S. Drennan was appointed Vice-President in succession to Mr. Weir. Instead of setting aside a fixed sum, as heretofore, for the purchase of Novels and light literature, it was this year ordered—

15th Feb. That the Committee be allowed discretionary power to purchase such Novels annually as, in their opinion, may be required, without restriction.

In connection with the adoption of the Free Libraries' Acts, and the proposed establishment of a Public Library in Belfast, suggestions were made and strongly supported at meetings of the Town Council, that the Belfast Library and Society for Promoting Knowledge should hand over its books and other property to the town authorities, to be converted into a Free Public Library for the use of the inhabitants.

In view of these suggestions, the Committee considered it desirable to make known their ideas on the proposal, and on April 5th it was accordingly moved by the Secretary, seconded by the Vice-President, and resolved unanimously, that—

5th April. As the Free Library Acts have been adopted, and are likely soon to become operative in Belfast, and as it has been openly proposed that the books and other property belonging to this Society should be handed over to the Free Library, the Committee think it right to state that no such power as that suggested is vested in them. In any case they consider that the Free Library will not interfere in any way with the working of this Library, and that within their respective lines there will be found ample room for both institutions in this town and neighbourhood. It is, therefore, their intention to give a cordial welcome to the Belfast Free Library as a fellow agent and helper in the cause for which this Society was founded ninety-five years ago—viz., "that of Promoting Knowledge."

At the same meeting it was

5th April. Ordered—That one copy of any book in great demand be retained in the Library, and lie upon the table for reading by the Members as long as it remains in special request.

It was decided to print 500 copies of the new Catalogue, and sell the same at 2s. 6d. The cost of each bound copy to the Society was stated to be 2s. 10¾d.

The balance sheet showed—Receipts, £641 5s. 8d.; Expenditure, £619 15s. 5d. Under the new arrangement the amount expended on fiction this year was £40 18s.

1884.

President—J. J. Murphy.   *Vice-President*—Dr. Drennan.   *Treasurer*—Thomas Montgomery.   *Secretary*—John Anderson.

15th May. Ordered—That the members of the British Medical Association, on the occasion of their Thirty-second Annual Meeting, to be held in Belfast in July next, be allowed Free Admission to this Library.

A presentation by Members and Subscribers was made to the Assistant-Librarian, Mr. Francis W. Knox, on his resigning his post; to which the President, Vice-President, and Secretary were directed to attach their names in token of the esteem in which he was held.

An application from the Bank of Ireland to have fifteen of their *employés* admitted to the privileges of Subscribers to the Library, on an annual payment of £10, was received; but the Committee, after deliberation, considered that the Rules of the Society precluded them from accepting the proposal. The matter was referred to a meeting of the Society at large, but, opinion being divided, no action was taken.

The balance sheet showed—Receipts, £654 2s. 10d.; Expenditure, £607 6s. 0d. (including Novels, £27 18s. 8d.)

1885.

President—J. J. Murphy. *Vice-President*—Dr. J. S. Drennan. *Treasurer*—Thomas Montgomery. *Secretary*—John Anderson.

On April 2nd it was resolved—

2nd April.   That £10 be contributed towards the illumination of the Linen Hall on the occasion of the intended visit of the Prince and Princess of Wales to Belfast.

In July it was reported that one of the weights of the clock in the tower, weighing 5 cwt., had fallen through the upper floor; but, as the accident occurred at night, no one was injured.

17th Dec.   Ordered—That the improvements suggested by Messrs. Young and Patterson regarding the ventilation of the rooms be carried out.

The balance sheet showed—Receipts, £734 4s. 1d.; Expenditure, £654 10s. 9d. (including Novels, £53 11s. 0d.)

1886.

President—J. J. Murphy. *Vice-President*—Dr. J. S. Drennan. *Treasurer*—Thomas Montgomery. *Secretary*—John Anderson.

18th Mar.   Ordered—That the name of the donor of any book presented to the Library be entered in such book, and that so far as possible in similar past presentations, the name of the donor be entered in the same way.

The large increase in the number of members and the rapid growth of the Library were found to involve a considerable increase of work on the part of the Committee, whose meetings had hitherto been held fortnightly. It was, therefore, resolved that in future the Committee should meet weekly, every Thursday, at eleven o'clock.

The new books, which, in accordance with a resolution of April, 1883, had hitherto lain on the table a fortnight before being put into circulation, were, in consequence of this new regulation, ordered to lie one week only, and then to be circulated.

The importance of preserving a record of the productions of the Presses of the Early Belfast Printers had for some time been recognised; and, in response to suggestions from various quarters, the Secretary this year undertook, with the co-operation of collectors and others interested in the matter, to prepare a List of Early Belfast Books, printed previous to the year 1751. His invitation for assistance was largely responded to, especially by the local librarians and collectors; and in October he was able to lay on the table the proof sheets of the Catalogue. The investigations necessary for the accomplishment of the work brought to light many interesting details connected with the old Belfast Printers, and revived to some extent an old controversy respecting the first Bible printed in Belfast, regarding which a copious note was appended to the Catalogue.

A hundred copies of the list were printed by order of the Committee, and sent to those who had assisted in the work, and to the newspapers. A second List was then commenced.

The balance sheet showed—Receipts, £784 4s. 5d.; Expenditure, £696 9s. 10d. (including Novels, £44 0s. 10d.).

1887-8.

President—Joseph J. Murphy, F.G.S. *Vice-President*—John S. Drennan, M.D. *Treasurer*—Thomas Montgomery, J.P. *Secretary*—John Anderson, J.P., F.G.S.

Committee—

Henry Burden, M.D.	Wm. H. Patterson, M.R.I.A.	James Wilson, M.E.
John F. Hodges, M.D., J.P.	Travers B. Smith	John Workman, J.P.
Robert MacAdam	Wm. Swanston, F.G.S.	Robert Young, C.E.
James O'Neill, M.A.	D. B. Walkington	

A Sub-Committee was appointed to ascertain from the Proprietors of the Linen Hall if they could give or let to the Committee a portion of the adjacent buildings on either side, the Society being considerably hampered for room in their present premises.

The Society had to lament the death of two of its active supporters during this year, and recorded the following resolutions on the Minutes:—

3rd Mar. Owing to the sudden death of the Rev. W. C. M'Cullagh, a much esteemed member of this Committee, it was resolved—That this meeting stand adjourned till this day week, and that the Secretary be instructed to communicate to the bereaved family a copy of this resolution.

10th Mar. That the Committee, having heard of the death of their fellow-member, Mr. Robert Jamieson, desire to place upon record their high appreciation of his services as a thorough worker in the interests of this Library, and their deep regret at the loss of one so much esteemed and respected by them all. That a copy of this resolution be sent to his widow, and that the meeting stand adjourned till this day week.

In response to an application from the Library, the Trustees of the British Museum presented the Society with a valuable package of books, containing twenty-eight volumes, three autotypes, and excerpts from their General Catalogue.

In May the following resolution was passed :—

12th May. As a practice had recently been introduced of proposing for purchase, time after time, books and periodicals that had been again and again

12th May, 1887. rejected by the Committee, and as such practice has given rise frequently to very unpleasant and unprofitable discussions, wasting time and obstructing business,

> Resolved—That in future, after the second rejection of any book or periodical by the Committee, should such be again proposed during the year, the proposal be treated in the same manner as books now are treated that are proposed, " to be ordered out of course"—that is to say, if ordered, it must be by the unanimous vote of the Members of Committee present and voting.

In view of the approaching Centenary of the Library, a feeling was expressed that some Record of its History would be appropriate to the occasion. It was suggested that such a work would be well done by the Rev. George Hill, of Holywood, who was accordingly requested to undertake it ; but as he was unable to comply with the wish of the Committee, the matter was referred to the Secretary.

The Society having received the offer of a further gift of Publications from the Record Office Commissioners, it was resolved—

10th Nov. That the Secretary be requested to write to the Lords of her Majesty's Treasury, thanking them for the grant to this Library, through Sir W. Ewart, Bart., M.P., of the whole or a part of the English and Irish Records Office Publications, and stating that the Committee would be glad to pay any expenses that may be incurred in forwarding to Belfast the packages containing the Books, and in returning the cases.

The Secretary (Mr. Anderson) was able, before the close of the year, to lay on the table the second and concluding part of his *Catalogue of Early Belfast-Printed Books*, bringing up the work to 1830. It was decided that the two parts be incorporated into one ; and 300 copies having been printed, it was agreed to send copies, as before, to all who had assisted in the work, as well as to the leading papers and public libraries—the remaining copies to be sold at one shilling each. It may be stated that this Catalogue records the titles of 1,155 books printed in Belfast between 1694 and 1830, of which number 938 have been inspected.

The Committee are glad to be able to point to the following Balance Sheet for this year as evidence that the last year of the first Century of the Society has been the most prosperous in its history :—

Balance Sheet, 1st January till 31st December, 1887.

December 31st.				January 31st.			
To Books and Periodicals purchased	£496	13	3	By Balance	£87	14	7
„ Binding, Printing, &c.	82	10	3	„ Subscriptions for the Year ...	709	15	4
„ Salaries and Gratuities... ...	185	12	6	„ One Life Member	11	11	0
„ Insurance ; also, Coal and Gas	37	18	1	„ Admission Fees...	11	11	0
„ Repairs, &c.	25	10	10	„ Periodicals, &c., Sold ...	26	19	10
„ Balance	22	18	11	„ Interest from Bank	3	12	1
	£851	3	10		£851	3	10

IN concluding this brief record of the rise and progress of the Library, a few observations on its present condition may not be out of place. After a century of varied growth, the Society of to-day is able to claim the possession of one of the most important public Libraries in Ireland.

Science.—Thanks to the wise policy of the original promoters, the foundation of the present collection was laid in works of sterling worth and solid value, without which no Library worthy of the name can claim to be complete. The Scientific portion of the Library, particularly, owes its excellence largely to the discrimination and judgment with which, in the early days of the Society, this department was attended to, and later on to the establishment of a special "Scientific Fund." Besides the Transactions of the learned Societies, and standard works representative of all branches of science, every effort was made to keep pace with the rapid advance of science by the purchase of modern books and editions; and the Committee hope that, should it be found possible to throw open this portion of the Library with fewer restrictions, it will be found fully adequate for all purposes of general reference.

Fine Arts.—In works relating to and illustrative of the Fine Arts, the Library, thanks also in no small degree to the wisdom of our predecessors, is well furnished. Among many treasures, we may be permitted to refer to such works as the fine set of Ruskin's works, Rowlandson's Caricatures, Bewick's illustrated works, Japanese ornaments and designs by Cutler, the choice specimens from Claude's "Liber Veritatis," and other picturesque and rare works. In this department also the Committee are alive to the importance of adding to their collection copies of the numerous finely illustrated works in which the Art of the present day is represented.

Irish Books.—A highly important and valuable portion of the Library is that devoted to books on the History and Literature of Ireland. The foregoing record contains several allusions to the interest which this branch of their collection excited in the minds of the early members, and it is gratifying to be able to point to the considerable and representative collection of works on Ireland at the present time on our shelves. The 300 or 400 Irish publications comprise almost all the important historical works relating to our own island, from the Annals of the Four Masters to the Transactions of the Archæological and Celtic Societies of recent years. In addition to these, the student of the Irish language is well furnished with grammars, dictionaries, &c., besides the best specimens of the native literature. It is hoped that, in view of the increasing rarity of books of this class, the collection already made may soon become still more complete.

G

Early Belfast Books.—In this connection attention may be once more directed to the rapidly increasing collection of locally printed books, which, as a result of the interest created by the recent publication of the Catalogue of Early Belfast Printed Books by this Society, has lately received special attention. In the Appendix to the Library Catalogue the titles of all such works in the possession of the Society have been collected in an easy form for reference, and it is not too much to hope that the Linen Hall Library may in the course of time become the repository of a copy of most, if not all, of the works bearing a Belfast imprint. Meanwhile, special attention is directed to the securing of works dealing with our local manufactures and industries.

Law, History, &c.—In works of History, Law, &c., the Library is amply provided, and here again the necessity of keeping pace with modern progress and ideas is fully recognised by the constant purchase of recent editions.

Books of Reference.—It has been the consistent policy of the Society to gather together a complete and comprehensive Reference Library, and in books of this nature the Library to-day is perhaps as well equipped as most of its kind. Standard works of reference on almost every subject are at the service of members, from the *Encyclopædia Britannica* downwards. Certainly not the least valuable works in this department are the complete files of our principal local newspapers, one of which at least—that of the *News-Letter*—is (though not absolutely complete) believed to be unique.

Belles Lettres.—Turning now to the less serious and more popular fields of literature, it may be stated that the *Belles Lettres* are fully represented, and occupy a large amount of space on the Society's shelves. All the chief classical works of English literature, in prose and verse, from Chaucer to the present day, are to be found there—many of them in several editions.

Fiction.—With regard to Fiction, it is only necessary to refer to the Catalogue and Appendix to see that in this department the Library is well and liberally supplied. The old stoutly-maintained rule of the Society against the introduction of all works of "trivial amusement" was slow in giving way to the demand from readers for works of this kind; but now the members have access to the best works in the whole range of imaginative and recreative literature.

Various Works.—In conclusion (without referring particularly to the other departments of literature and art—as, for instance, Travels, Politics, Foreign Writers, Biographies, &c.), the Committee feel that they have reason to be proud of the collection of books—now exceeding 25,000 Volumes—under their care; and their desire is that every one of the 836 Members of the Society may be induced to avail himself more fully of his privileges, and acquaint himself with the extent and value of the Library whose Centenary is this day celebrated.

LINEN HALL LIBRARY,

BELFAST, 13th May, 1888.

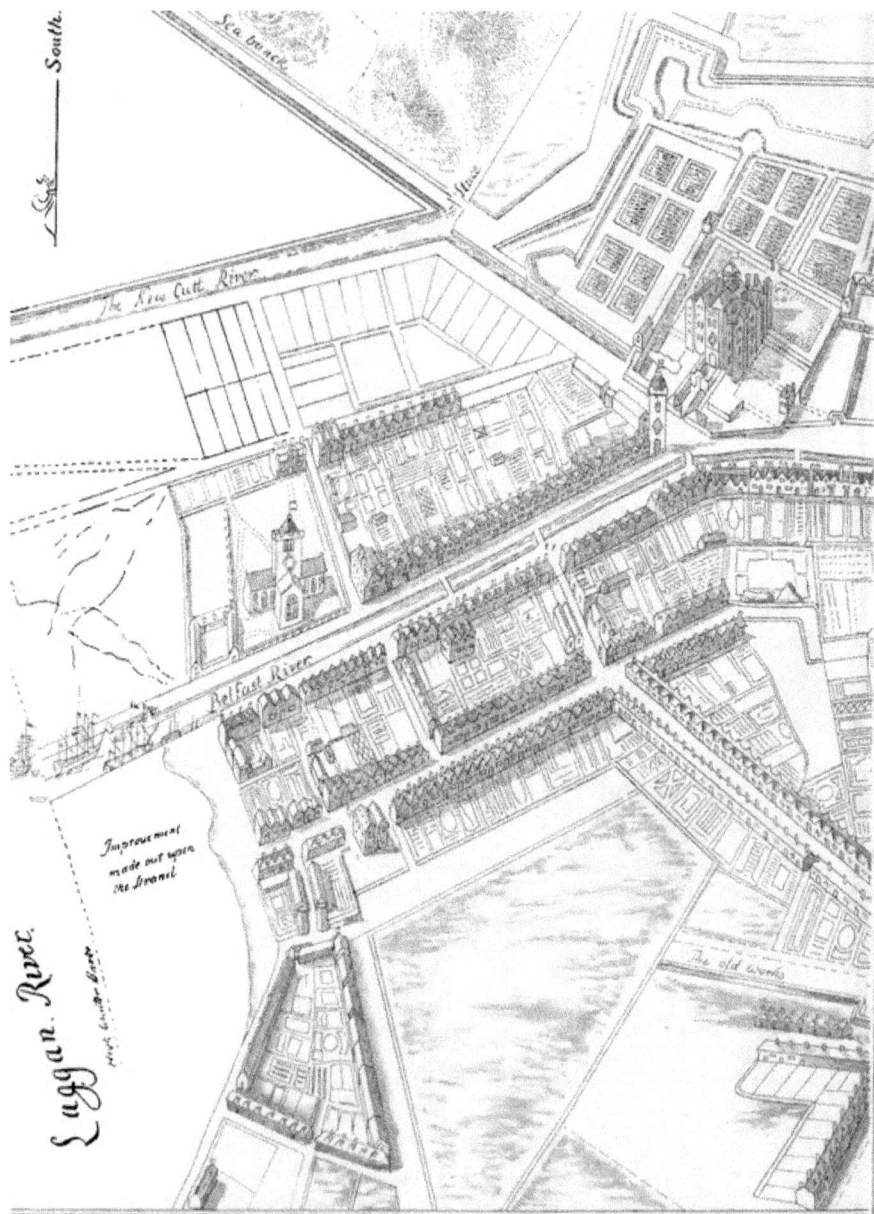

South.

Scale

Sea bank

Slou

The New Cutt River

Belfast River

Luggan River

with turn ditt

Improvement
made out upon
the Strand

The old works

Ground Plan of Belfast

The Ground Plan of Belfast
Sʳ Tho. Phillips
Anno
1685
Copied by H.S.Barton. 1860.

A Scale Containing one Thousand feet

Appendix A.

Copy of the Resolutions in favour of Catholic Emancipation, passed by the Society on January 17th, 1792. — *(Extract from Minutes.)*

IN consequence of a requisition from several members, a meeting of the Society was called on Thursday, January 26th, 1792—the Rev. JAMES BRYSON in the chair.

A motion was made and carried on the propriety of their publicly declaring their sentiments on the great and important question of admitting the Roman Catholics to a full and immediate participation of the rights enjoyed by their fellow-citizens and countrymen.

26th Jan., 1792.   Resolved—That the Rev. James Bryson, Robert M'Cormick, James M'Cormick, Æneas Lamont, and James De Butts, as Secretary, be appointed a Committee for the purpose of writing a paper expressive of our desire that such a measure may be carried into effect.

Resolved—That the Society meet To-morrow Evening, in Brown's, to hear the report of their Committee.

At a meeting of the Society on Friday evening, January 27th, 1792, the following resolutions were unanimously agreed to :—

27th Jan., 1792.   1st. Resolved—That civil and religious liberty is the birthright of every human being; that Governments were formed to secure them in the possession of these rights, and that States should be regulated so as to protect them in the exercise of it.

2nd. That doctrines of faith and modes of worship can neither give nor take away the rights of men; because opinion is not the Object of Government; because the mode of expressing Religious Worship ought to be left to the judgment of God and the decision of conscience; and because persecution, however it be disguised, is destructive of the equality of men and the most sacred laws of nature.

3rd. That, while we rejoice with every virtuous and enlightened mind at the rapid progress which these principles have lately made, and the Illustrious events to which their happy Influence has given birth—Events which are the proudest boast of human nature, and which will supply history with ornaments unknown to former ages[1]—it is with inexpressible regret that we behold their circumscribed operation in this our native land.

4th. That Ireland can never deserve the name of a free State while a great majority of her Inhabitants enjoy the rights of citizens in so partial a manner; while they are totaly Governed by the will of others; in a word,

---

(1). Referring evidently to the recent American and French Revolutions.

27th Jan., 1792. while they are unjustly excluded from all share in the making and the administration of the laws under which they live.

5th. In fine, it is our most fervent wish that the nation would call for their deliverance with a voice so temperate as to excite no tumult; so affectionate as to conciliate the hearts of all; but so *United* and so *powerfull* as to carry conviction to every source of legislation.

Resolved—That the above resolutions be published in the Belfast Papers.

JAMES M'CORMICK, *Chairman.*

Appendix B.

Copy of the Resolution in Favour of a Free School, passed unanimously by the Society on April 3rd, 1794, on the motion of Dr. White :—

3rd April, 1794.　　The importance of Education to every member of society is so obvious to the most superficial observer that it appears altogether unnecessary to use any arguments to enforce its utility. Nevertheless, by far the greater part of every society is totally deprived of the slightest advantages of education, and consequently, though essential to the well-being of all Ranks of Mankind, have it not in their power to contribute so much to the general good as could be wished and might be expected. To impress on the mind in the early period of life sound principles of morality, habits of application, and a desire of information (among the lower order of society), would, in an eminent degree, contribute to the welfare and happiness of the individual, and of the community to which he belongs. The number of people in this town who have it not in their power to obtain the slenderest rudiments of education is very considerable, and the feeble attempts which have been made here, as well as in other places, to remedy this evil by the Institution of Sunday Schools appears to have been totally inadequate. One day in the week spent in education would enable the brightest genius only to make a slow and inconsiderable progress in literary acquirements, and as superior capacity falls to the lot of few, those of common abilities would scarcely receive any benefit. Besides, the view of the institution of Sunday Schools seems generally to have been limited to reading only. The object of this Society is to embrace a plan of education of infinitely more extent and importance, viz. :—Reading, Writing, Spelling, Arithmetic, and possibly in some cases a portion of Mathematics. How important such an establishment might be to society it is hardly necessary to say; it would produce useful mechanics and artificers of all sorts ; it would furnish a useful nursery for sailors ; it would produce such a change in morals, such diligence, application, and abilities in every pursuit, that it would bid fair eventually to supersede some of the other charitable institutions of this town, which are infinitely more expensive. It might in the end untenant your poorhouse. This Society does therefore resolve, agreeably to the spirit of its association, to use its influence and patronage in establishing in this town a " Free School" on a liberal principle for the purpose above mentioned, and they entertain no doubt that an adequate fund may be raised from the well disposed and wealthy inhabitants of the town of Belfast to enable them to carry the scheme into execution.

APPENDIX C.

A List of the Officers and Members of Committee of the Belfast Library and Society for Promoting Knowledge, from 1788 to 1888.

(The date indicates the year when each person was first appointed.)

Presidents:

1792 Dr. Alex. Haliday	1828 Dr. Robert Tennent	1869 Dr. William M'Gee
1798 Rev. Dr. Wm. Bruce	1837 Rev. Wm. Bruce	1874 Joseph John Murphy
1817 Rev. Dr. S. M. Stephenson		

Vice-Presidents:

1792 Robert Bradshaw	1814 Rev.Dr.S.M.Stephenson	1838 Rev. Wm. Cairns
1794 Rev. Dr. Wm. Bruce	1817 James Ferguson	1840 William Thompson
1798 Rev. Patrick Vance	1824 Dr. Robert Tennent	1853 Dr. William M'Gee
1800 John Holmes	1828 Dr. Saml. S. Thomson	1869 Joseph John Murphy
1801 Robert Holmes	1832 Rev. Dr. T. D. Hincks	1874 Arthur C. Weir
1802 Rev.Dr.S.M.Stephenson	1837 William Thompson	1883 Dr. J. S. Drennan
1813 Dr. William Drennan		

Secretaries:

1788 James De Butts	1794 Robert Simms	1833 Maurice Cross
1792 Robert M'Cormick	1796 Gilbert M'Ilveen, Jr.	1836 Dr. Kidley
1793 William Clarke	1797 James Munfoad	1852 Robert Gray
1793 Geo. B. Madden	1802 Thomas M'Donnell	1852 William Browne
1794 John Templeton	1808 James Munfoad	1873 John Anderson

Treasurers:[1]

1793 John Holmes	1838 Wm. T. Harvey	1875 James T. Bristow
1808 James Munfoad	1842 Wm. Bottomley	1878 Thomas Montgomery
1829 Wm. Suffern		

Librarians:

1792 Robert Cary	1821 William M'Clure	1837 James Stewart
1794 Thomas Russell	1823 Alexander Henderson	1868 Joseph Stephens
1796 John M'Coughtry	1829 James Munfoad	1871 Joseph Watson
1802 James Sloan	1829 Alexander Neilson	1872 Francis A. Maitland
1817 Robert Sloan	1830 George M'Ewen	

(1). At various periods in the early history of the Society the duties of Treasurer were undertaken by the Secretary.

Members of Committee :

1791 Robert M'Cormick	1794 Counsellor Sampson	1802 David Bigger
James M'Cormick	Thomas Cruise	1803 James M'Adam
Maurice Spottiswood	James Ferguson	James Orr[3]
Robert Cary	1795 Samuel M'Tier[1]	Dr. Blackwood
John Rabb	John M'Coughtry	Rev. Dr. W. H. Drummond
1792 Rev. James Bryson	Samuel Neilson	Valentine Jones[4]
Dr. M'Donnell	John Templeton	1805 Wm. Auchinleck[5]
James Cunningham	Henry Joy M'Cracken	Wm. Tucker
Hugh M'Nemara	Gilbert M'Ilveen, jun.	Wm. Clarke
John Bradshaw	Rev. Hugh O'Donnell,	1806 Rev. Edward May[6]
Æneas Lamont	P.P.	John Sinclaire[7]
Robert Callwell	Wm. Tennent	1807 Rainey Maxwell
John Haslett	1796 Thomas Biggs	Dr. Purdon
William Hamilton	Dr. Scott	Wm. T. Harvey
Alexander Boyd	James Hyndman	1808 Dr. William Drennan
1793 Rev. Dr. Wm. Bruce	1797 James Munfoad	1809 Rev. Edward Groves
Rev. John Clarke	1798 Robert Telfair	1810 Dr. Marshall
Henry Joy	John Houston	Rev. W. St. John Smith
George B. Madden	John S. Ferguson	Alex. Mitchell
Robert Simms	1799 Robert Bailie	1811 Robert Tennent
1794 Dr. John C. White	Thomas M'Donnell	1812 Wm. H. Ferrar
Robert Holmes	1800 James M'Cleery	1813 Rev. Dr. Wm. Crolly, P.P.
Robert Getty	Dr. Wm. Haliday	Hugh Magill
Rev. Sinclaire Kelburn	Rev. Robert Acheson	Peter M'Gouran
Rev. Patrick Vance	Rev. W. J. Smyth	William Sloan
Robert Bradshaw	1801 Christopher Salmon	Robert MacAdam
Dr. Moore	1802 Dr. Saml. S. Thomson	1814 Rev. Mr. O'Bierne
Wm Sinclaire	John Gregg[2]	1817 Rev. Wm. Bruce

(1). Was called to the chair at a meeting of the inhabitants in October, 1792, at which a series of resolutions was passed expressive of sympathy with "the French National Convention." In the evening the town was illuminated.

(2). Had been Clerk to the Irish House of Lords till the Union. A liberal contributor to the local charities. He was supposed to be the donor of two £500 notes put upon a plate after a charity sermon by Dr. Hanna, in Rosemary Street, on the 29th October, 1820.

(3). Director of the Northern Bank; father of Lady Cranbrook.

(4). West Indian and wine merchant; an active and generous supporter of all the charitable institutions in the town. He died at the great age of 94.

(5). Author of *Interest Tables* and other mercantile works. He was a kinsman of our respected townsman, W. A. Robinson, Esq., J.P., stockbroker, &c.

(6). Brother to the Marchioness of Donegall, and father of the present Lord Chief Justice May. He was originally agent for the Donegall estate, and subsequently took orders, and became Rector of Belfast.

(7). Linen merchant and bleacher, and an ardent lover of field sports; one of the first Volunteers of the eighteenth century. He died at the great age of 94.

Members of Committee.—*(Continued.)*

1817 William Boyd	1838 Rev. John Porter	1862 Robert MacAdam
Francis Johnson	Arthur K. Miller	Dr. R. F. Dill
Rev. W. D. H. M'Ewen	1839 Rev. Dr. J. Seaton Reid	1863 Thomas L'Estrange
Rev. Saml. Hanna, D.D.	James M'Adam, jun.	1864 Rev. Dr. Killen
1818 Dr. William Knight	1840 William Bottomley	Henry Reid
Dr. Robert M'Cluney	1841 Thomas M'Clure[2]	1865 Rev. Wm. MacIlwaine,
1823 Lawson Annesley	Rev. Dr. Robert Wilson	D.D.
1824 Rev. Prof. Wm. Cairns	1842 William Dunville	John Workman
Prof. James Thomson	John Grattan	John Anderson
1825 Rev. Dr. R. J. Bryce	Dr. Burden	Rev. W. C. M'Cullagh
1826 Dr. Young	1843 Edmund Getty	Rev. Robert Workman
1827 Rev. A. C. Macartney[1]	1845 Henry Garrett	Dr. Saml. Browne, R.N.
1828 Drummond Anderson	1847 William Ferguson	1866 William D. Henderson
John B. Shannon	Dr. John S. Drennan	Wm. Edmund Crothers
William Turner	Dr. T. Andrews, F.R.S.	Dr. J. Leslie Porter
William Suffern	Thomas Chermside	1869 John Corry
John M'Adam	1848 Dr. John F. Hodges	1873 Charles Druitt
John Montgomery	1849 George K. Smith	1874 W. H. Patterson
Valentine Whitla[3]	1851 Professor Craik	1875 James T. Bristow
Robert Simms, jun.	1852 Robert Gray	1878 Thomas Montgomery
1830 Professor Stevelly	1853 Rev. Dr. M'Cosh	1879 W. A. Robinson
1832 Dr. Kidley	1854 Robert Taylor	Robert MacGeagh
John Macartney	1855 Joseph John Murphy	1883 D. B. Walkington
1834 William Sinclair	1856 Dr. Dickie	James Wilson
1835 William Thompson	Alex. Montgomery	1884 Geo. T. Glover
1836 William Webb	1858 Arthur C. Weir	1885 Robert Jamieson
Robert Jas. Tennent	1859 Rev. James Young	T. B. Smith
1837 Samuel G. Fenton	William Browne	1886 William Swanston
Dr. Wm. M'Gee	William M'Ilwrath	1887 James O'Neill, M.A.
Dr. Jas. L. Drummond	1860 Robert Young, C.E.	Dr. Henry Burden

(1). Vicar of Belfast for many years; previously served as a Captain in the Royal Artillery throughout the Peninsular War.

(2). For many years Chairman of the Harbour Commissioners. He was also Founder of Stanhope Street Schools, Incorporated 1887.

(3). Now Sir Thomas M'Clure, Bart., formerly M.P. for Belfast and for Londonderry County; also, V.L. for County Down.

APPENDIX D.

TABLE showing the Receipts, Expenditure, Amount Paid for Books, and No. of Proprietors, Members, and Subscribers during the years in which a financial report was presented. Also, amount paid towards Scientific Fund and for Books had on Loan :—

Year.	Receipts.			Expenditure.			Paid for Books.			No. of Proprietors, Members and Subscribers, if noted.
	£	s.	d.	£	s.	d.	£	s.	d.	
1828	213	19	3	172	18	10	66	4	3	152
1829	213	19	3	209	17	3	113	18	11	150
1830	144	9	10	144	5	1½	69	12	3	158
1831(1)	171	10	8½	114	2	9	51	10	3	155
1832	231	17	5	152	3	0	79	19	8	145
1833	279	1	7	214	0	6	123	2	1	156
1834	262	19	7	232	17	2	157	7	5	168
1835	215	10	5	155	8	1	73	6	4	169
1836	270	16	1	177	0	8	94	0	3	178
1837	292	6	10	227	10	10	146	16	4	177
1838	272	6	11	283	4	11	140	19	4	179
1839	195	10	0	154	16	7	47	2	7	176
1840	245	3	5	252	5	1	132	15	2	178
1841	174	0	1	133	19	1	38	4	10	165
1842	239	6	3	270	3	5	129	16	0	189
1843	195	14	9	232	3	8	73	17	0	180
1844	219	7	0	203	11	2½	56	1	6	......
1845	218	19	5	218	19	3	69	16	11	......
1846	195	18	6	206	11	7	73	6	3	......
1847	191	19	6	198	9	1	77	6	2	......
1848	192	12	7	193	16	3	85	0	8	......
1849	210	2	10	172	10	1	73	9	2	......
1850	....			....			....			......
1851	....			....			....			199
1852	208	1	6	188	19	9	73	9	3	......
1853	220	12	7	212	4	6	117	17	2	......
1854	216	12	11	200	12	0	92	3	5	......
1855	212	9	11	223	19	7	126	17	3	......
1856	239	16	6	244	2	9	134	1	6	......
1857	....			....			....			......

(1). Receipts diminished by £34 11s. 7d., the defalcations of the late Librarian.

Year.	Receipts.			Expenditure.			Paid for Books.			No. of Proprietors, Members and Subscribers, if noted.
	£	s.	D.	£	s.	D.	£	s.	D.	
1858	....			....			....			233[1]
1859	....			....			....			......
1860	323	19	6	255	14	0	127	13	1	......
1861	....			....			....			......
1862	219	11	7	220	1	3	105	18	11	......
1863	225	9	8	226	9	4	91	6	11	......
1864	222	11	11	206	6	6	68	8	2	......
1865	305	11	4	244	13	0	86	9	5	......
1866	385	10	2	338	12	6	127	2	9	......
1867	373	13	3	339	1	8	122	16	10	......
1868	355	17	11	288	7	1	103	0	11	......
1869	377	10	4	341	0	5	131	7	7	......
1870	364	8	11	319	15	11	97	16	0	......
1871	369	1	11	338	17	0	97	17	10	......
1872	401	18	4	369	12	3	93	2	6	......
1873	445	10	3	438	13	6	136	16	10	402[2]
1874	457	18	5	451	3	4	156	19	6	......
1875	458	3	6	437	12	1	177	6	10	......
1876	489	1	4	461	19	3	201	4	8	......
1877	515	16	5	498	4	2	223	10	7	......
1878	515	17	3	492	3	1	232	0	11	......
1879	557	10	6	539	7	9	230	6	5	......
1880	578	14	9	561	2	11	253	18	6	......
1881	608	19	9	592	4	10	310	5	3	......
1882	617	15	1	596	13	0	212	2	7	......
1883	641	5	8	619	15	5	273	13	10	......
1884	654	2	10	607	6	0	317	0	10	......
1885	734	4	1	654	10	9	336	7	1	......
1886	784	4	5	696	9	10	352	8	8	......
1887	851	3	10	828	4	11	406	13	3	836[3]

Amount paid towards Scientific Fund, 1837-1849   ... £210 3 1

     Do.   by Special Subscription, 1837-1849 ..   210 3 1

                                            £420 6 2

Amount paid by the Society for Books had on Loan, 1863-1872 ...   ... 483 19 8

     (1). Proprietors 67
          Members 67
          Annual Guinea Subscribers (for the first time recorded) ... 99—233
     (2). Proprietors 65
          Members 87
          Annual Guinea Subscribers 189
          Do.   Half Guinea do. ... ... 61—402
     (3). Proprietors 64
          Members 199
          Annual Guinea Subscribers 555
          Do.   Half Guinea do. ... ... 18—836

Appendix E.

List of the Principal Benefactions to the Library since 1800.[1]

1803	Nicholas Grimshaw...	Six copies of his Pamphlet.
1805	Major Thompson ...	Code des Loix.
1807	John Templeton ...	Index to Ten volumes Botanical Magazine.
1811	Dr. Anderson, Edinburgh ...	His Life of Smollet.
1812	Wm. H. Ferrar ...	History of Limerick. By J. Ferrar.
1817	Record Commissioners	Reports, &c., 1810 to 1825.
1819	Wm. Sloan ...	Map of the County Londonderry.
1823	Rev. Dr. T. D. Hincks	Reports on Bogs of Ireland, 3 vols.
1824	George Ensor ...	Seven volumes, 8vo, useful Books.
1830	Royal Irish Academy ...	Transactions, 16 vols.
1831	Dr. Henry MacCormac ...	102 volumes, various.
	Do. ...	Pamphlets on various subjects.
	Do.	File of Sierra Leone Newspapers.
	Do.	File of miscellaneous American Newspapers.
1832	Anna Maria Winter	Thoughts on the Moral Order of Nature, 2 copies.
	Rev. Dr. T. D. Hincks	Statistics of Roscommon (Griffiths), Tyrone, and Antrim Collieries.
1835	Dr. S. S. Thomson ...	A lot of Pamphlets.
1836	Dr. Bruce ...	Two volumes of his Works.
1837	C. Howard (Secretary to Admiralty) ...	Books.
1838	Record Office Commissioners	Several valuable Works.
	Rev. Dr. T. D. Hincks ...	His Works.
1839	Captain Portlock ...	Surveys and Address to the Geological Society.
1840	T. D. Wyse, M.P. ...	Speech on Education.
1841	Earl of Enniskillen	Parliamentary Reports.
1845	John Henderson, Glasgow...	On Christian Union.
1846	Rev. Dr. T. D. Hincks ...	Valpy's Delphin Classics, 157 vols.
1848	Dr. John S. Drennan ...	His father's Fugitive Pieces.
1849	Sir H. De la Beche ...	Memoirs, Geological Survey of Great Britain.
1851	Rev. W. Bruce ...	Two Greek Books.
1852	Rev. Dr. T. D. Hincks ...	Royal Irish Academy's Proceedings, Vol. IV.
	Do. ...	Journal of the Statistical Society of London.
	Do. ...	Neilson's Irish Grammar.
	Do. ...	Jukes' Excursions about Newfoundland.

(1). A List of Benefactors prior to 1800 is given at pp. 21-22.

1853	Rev. Dr. Edward Hincks ...	His Works on the Assyrio-Babylonian Phonetic Characters.
1854	Rev. Dr. Abraham Hume ...	Proceedings of the Historic Society of Lancashire and Yorkshire.
1855	Sir Roderick Murchison ...	Several Scientific Works.
1859	Jas. Alex. Henderson ...	*News-Letter* for years 1835, 1838, 1839, 1840.
1861	Sir James Emerson Tennent	Publications of the Meteorological Department.
1865	Rev. Dr. Reeves	His Work on the Culdees of the British Islands.
	Dr. Young (American Consul)	Diplomatic Correspondence.
	George Hughes	O'Reilly's Irish-English Dictionary.
	Dr. James Moore	Proceedings Royal Irish Academy, 8 parts.
1867	Dr. Wm. M'Gee	Text Book to Turrets and Tripod Systems. By Cole.
1868	James Greaves	Religious Works, 46 vols.
	Wm. Steele Nicholson ...	Life of St. Patrick.
	Dr. Wm. M'Gee	Life of Thomas D'Arcy M'Gee ; and a Pamphlet on Specie in Canada, by Hon. Isaac Buchanan.
	Colonel Smythe	A Notice of the New Church of St. Patrick, Jordanstown.
		Genesis of the Angels. (Secretary instructed to acknowledge the receipt of. By whom presented not mentioned).
1869	Thomas M'Clure	Commission Report on the Established Church. 1868.
	Surgeon-Major Bacot ...	A Sketch of the Bahamas. By himself.
	J. S. Bateman	Description of the Proposed Railway between England and France.
1870	The Meteorological Society	Records.
	A. Fitzgibbon, Stoneyford ...	A Copy of Unpublished Geraldine Documents.
1871	Miss Cunningham, Macedon	Books, Papers, and Pamphlets.
	Dr. James Bryce ... , ...	The Geology of Edinburgh and Neighbourhood.
	Rev. G. T. Payne	A Narrative on Witchcraft in Island Magee.
	Rev. Dr. A. Hume... ...	Transactions of the Historical Society of Lancashire and Cheshire.
1872	W. H. Patterson	Assembly's Shorter Catechism.
	Dr. Wm. M'Gee	Private Correspondence of Thomas Raikes with the Duke of Wellington.
1873	Henry Bruce	Rinuccini's Embassy in Ireland, 1645-9.
1875	George Hughes	Pamphlet entitled—Linen : its Virtues and Advantages. Also, 3 vols. of Contemporary Review (which were not in Library).
	The Royal Irish Academy...	Portions of Vols. 24 and 25, to complete set.
	Robert Young	Ossian and the Clyde. By P. H. Waddell.

1876	C. Druitt	Report of the British Association in Belfast, 1875.
	J. J. Murphy	Report of the Royal Commission on Vivisection.
1877	George Glover	Report of the British Association for 1875.
	Prof. Everett	Copy of his Work on Shorthand.
1878	Counsellor Gibson	A Set of National Education Reports.
	M'Caw, Stevenson & Orr ...	Jottings on Current English. By "Democritus."
	Rev. Dr. MacIlwaine ...	Lyra Hibernica Sacra. By himself.
	Rev. Dr. A. Hume... ...	Remarks on the Irish Dialect of the English Language.
	Do.	A Volume of the Transactions "Historical Society of Lancashire and Cheshire."
1879	M'Caw, Stevenson & Orr	A Talk about Bishops. By T. L. Scott.
	Do.	A King's Daughter and other Poems. By S. R. Keightley.
	Do.	The Murmur of the Shells. By S. K. Cowan.
	William Sharp, M.D. ...	Humanity and the Man.
	Henry Bruce	Ulster Civil War, 1641. By John M'Donnell.
	Rev. T. M. Gorman ...	Christian Psychology. By himself.
1880	Wm. Hodgson	(By bequest, through Mr. Charles Elcock,) his Work, entitled, Society of Friends in the 19th Century. 2 vols.
1881	Robert Jamieson	His Work on Political Economy.
	Dr. Henry MacCormac ...	Language and its Study. By W. D. Whitney. On Phthisis and the Supposed Influence of Climate. By W. Thomson. Consumption and the Breath Re-breathed. By himself (Dr. MacCormac).
	Henry Bruce	Copy of Report of the Commissioners of Inquiry into the Working of the Landlord and Tenants' Act, 1870 (Ireland).
	James O'Neill, M.A. ...	The Siege of Derry, by Graham.
	Professor Major	Seven Sermons by Robert Russell. *Belfast*, 1751.
1882	A. Fitzgibbon	Series of the Geraldine Documents.
	John Anderson	Juvenile Poems. By Thomas Romney Robinson. *Belfast*, 1806.
	William Swanston	Set of Reports Belfast Naturalists' Field Club.
1884	Professor Everett	King's Briefs.
	Do.	An Outline of Hindustani Language.
	James O'Neill, M.A. ...	History General Hospital, Belfast.
	Dr. Esler	Guide to Belfast.
1885	Rev. Alexander Gordon ...	Sermon by James Duchal, printed in Belfast, 1736.
	Royal Academical Institution	Eight valuable Old Works.

1885	Dr. J. S. Drennan	Glendalough, &c., by late Dr. Drennan and Sons.
	William Swanston	Drummond's Letter to a Young Naturalist.
1886	Edward Ellis	Irish Education Directory. By himself.
	The Lord Lieutenant (Earl Aberdeen)	Ordnance Maps of Antrim and Down, 6-inch scale.
	Francis J. Bigger ...	Select Papers of the Belfast Literary Society.
	Dr. M'Donnell	The Light of History on Irish Measures, 1580-1641.
	Henry Bradshaw[1]	The Experienced Huntsman. *Belfast,* 1714.
	Do.	Life and Acts of Sir Wm. Wallace. *Belfast,* 1728.
	The Right Rev. Dr. Reeves	Memoir of the Public Library at Armagh.
	Henry Dix Hutton	Three Books on Library Work.
	James Wilson	Proctor's Atlas of the Stars.
1887	L. M. Ewart	The Gazetteer, or Newsman's Interpreter. *Belfast,* 1740.
	The British Museum ...	Fifty volumes of valuable Works.
	J. M. Sloan	The Phonograph Instructor.
	Librarian, Queen's College	Classified Catalogue of Books in the Library.
	James Jenkins ...	Jamison's Political Economy.
	Do.	Jamison's Richard Cobden.
	Do.	Jamison's Robert Burns in his Youth.
	James O'Neill, M.A. ...	The Year of Grace.
	Do.	Sheridan's Dictionary of the English Language.
	Dr. William Frazer... ...	The Remains of St. Mary's Abbey.
	Countess of Dalhousie ...	Memoirs of Count Guiseppe Pasolini.
	Travers B. Smith	History of the First Presbyterian Congregation, Belfast.
	John Campbell ...	Do. do.
	Robert Young ...	The Victorian Year.
	John Anderson	Juvenile Poems, by Robert Sullivan. *Belfast,* 1818.

(1). University Librarian at Cambridge. He was connected by birth with Ulster, and took great interest in the formation of the recent Catalogue of *Early Belfast Printed Books.*

APPENDIX F.

Chronological List of Catalogues, as issued by the Belfast Society for Promoting Knowledge, of which Copies exist, or the publication of which is recorded on the Minutes:—

1793—Rules of the Belfast Society for Promoting Knowledge, with a Catalogue of the Books. Belfast: 1793.
    No copy known.

1794—Catalogue of the Books of the Belfast Society for Promoting Knowledge. Belfast : 1794.

> *No copy known.*

1794—Catalogue of Scientific Apparatus of the Belfast Society for Promoting Knowledge. Belfast : 1794.

> *No copy known.*

1806—Appendix to the Catalogue. *Belfast: Printed by Smyth & Lyons.* 1806. 12mo ; pp. 12.

1808—Rules of the Belfast Society for Promoting Knowledge, with a Catalogue of the Books. *Belfast: Printed by Smyth & Lyons.* 1808. 8vo ; pp. 47, viz.:— 1-12, The Laws ; 13-46, Catalogue ; 47, Broken Sets.

1811—An Appendix to the Catalogue of Books of the Society for Promoting Knowledge. *Belfast: Printed by D. & S. Lyons, No. 1, Corn Market.* 1811. 8vo ; pp. 10.

1814—Rules of the Belfast Society for Promoting Knowledge, with a Catalogue of the Books. *Belfast: Printed by Alexander Mackay, " News-Letter " Office.* 1814. Sm. 4to ; pp. 68, viz.:—1-12, Rules ; 13-66, Catalogue ; 67, Broken Sets ; 68, Additions. The Catalogue is printed and paged on one side of the leaf only.

1818—Appendix to the Catalogue of 1814 of the Books of the Belfast Society for Promoting Knowledge. February, 1818. *Belfast: Printed by Alexander Mackay, " News-Letter " Office, Bridge Street.* 12mo ; pp. 12, viz.:—1-11, Appendix to Catalogue ; 12, Rules in addition to those in the Catalogue of 1814.

1819—Rules of the Belfast Society for Promoting Knowledge, with a Catalogue of the Books. *Belfast: Printed by Lyons.* 1819. 12mo; pp. 119, viz. :—1-15, The Laws ; 17-83, Alphabetical Catalogue of the Books, Charts, &c. ; 85-116, Classified Catalogue (of a portion of the Books only); 117, Additions since printing ; 118, Broken Sets ; 119, Maps, &c.

1822—Appendix to the Catalogue of 1819 of the Books of the Belfast Society for Promoting Knowledge. *Belfast: Printed by Joseph Smyth.* 1822. 12mo; pp. 9.

1825—Laws of the Belfast Society for Promoting Knowledge, with a General Catalogue of the Books, Maps, &c. ; to which is subjoined—for the greater ease of reference—a Classified Catalogue relating to some particular subjects. *Belfast: Printed by Joseph Smyth, 34, High Street.* 1825. 12mo; pp. 72, viz.:— 1-8, The Laws ; 9-47, Alphabetical Catalogue ; 48-70, Classified Catalogue ; 71, Broken Sets ; 72, Maps, &c.

1829—Appendix to the Catalogue of Books of 1825 belonging to the Belfast Society for Promoting Knowledge. *Belfast: Printed by Thomas Mairs, Joy's Court.* 1829. 12mo ; pp. 10.

1836—Catalogue of the Belfast Library and Society for Promoting Knowledge. Belfast : 1836.

> *No copy known.*

1839—Appendix to the Catalogue of Books of 1836 belonging to the Belfast Society for
    Promoting Knowledge. Belfast: 1839.
        No copy known.
1843—Catalogue of the Belfast Library and Society for Promoting Knowledge. Belfast:
    1843.
        No copy known.
1851—Catalogue of the Belfast Library and Society for Promoting Knowledge, White
    Linen Hall. *Belfast: Printed by Robert & Daniel Read, Crown Entry*, 1851.
    8vo; pp. x., 134, viz.:—i.-x., The Laws; 1-101, Alphabetical Catalogue; 102-
    123, Classified Index; 124-5, Appendix; 126-128, List of Members and Officers;
    129-134, Books purchased from the Scientific Fund of the Library.
1858—Supplement to the Catalogue of the Belfast Library, containing the Books received
    from 1851 up to the month of July, 1858. *Belfast: Printed by Alexander
    Mayne, High Street*, 1858. 8vo; pp. 32, viz.:—2, List of Officers for 1858;
    3-27, Supplement to Catalogue; 28-29, List of Members and Shareholders;
    30, List of Annual Subscribers, 31-32, Balance Sheets for 1856-1857.
1861—Catalogue of the Belfast Library and Society for Promoting Knowledge. *Belfast:
    Printed by Alexander Mayne*, 1861. 500 copies ordered.
1871—Catalogue of the Belfast Library and Society for Promoting Knowledge. *Belfast:
    Printed at the "News-Letter" Office*, 1871. 8vo; pp. 222.
1871-9—Supplements to the Catalogue of the Belfast Library and Society for Promoting
    Knowledge, of 1871, viz.:—
        June, 1871, to March, 1876. 50 pp., 8vo.
        April, 1876, to June, 1877. 12 pp., 8vo.
        June, 1877, to Dec., 1877. 8 pp., 8vo.
        Jan., 1878, to Dec., 1878. 14 pp., 8vo.
        Jan., 1879, to Dec., 1879. 16 pp., 8vo.
1883—Belfast Library and Society for Promoting Knowledge. Founded in the year 1788.
    Laws, Regulations, and Catalogue of the Library, White Linen Hall. *Belfast:
    Printed by Alexander Mayne, Corporation Street, &c.*, 1883. 8vo; pp. xii., 384,
    viz.:—i.-xii., Laws, Regulations, &c.; 1-294, Catalogue; 295-339, Light Litera-
    ture alphabetically arranged according to Authors; 340-384, The same, accord-
    ing to Titles.
1887—Supplement, from January, 1883, till December, 1886. *Belfast: Printed by
    Alexander Mayne*. 1887. 8vo; pp. 88, viz.:—1-43, Supplement to Catalogue;
    44-66, Supplement to Light Literature, alphabetically arranged according to
    Authors; 67-88, The same, according to Titles. Under "*Belfast*" is given a
    List of all the Belfast-printed Books in the Library.

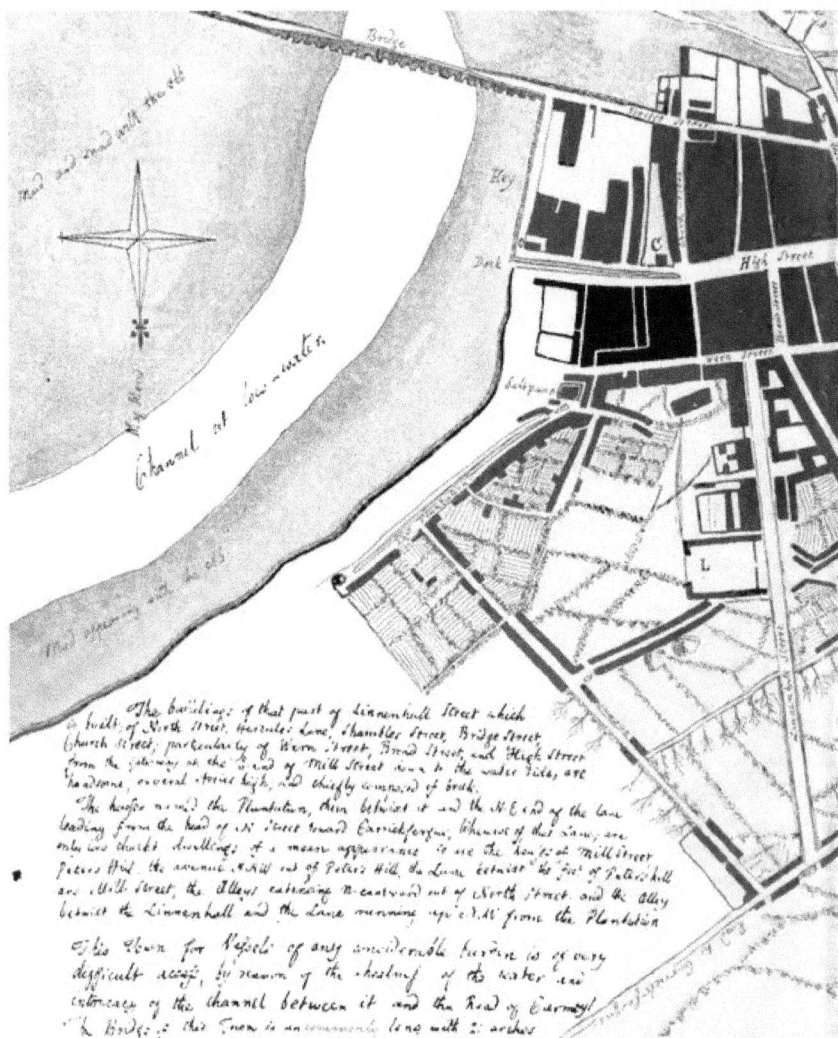

Map of Belfast, 1757.

Fac-simile of an Original Drawing recently discove
by permission of L

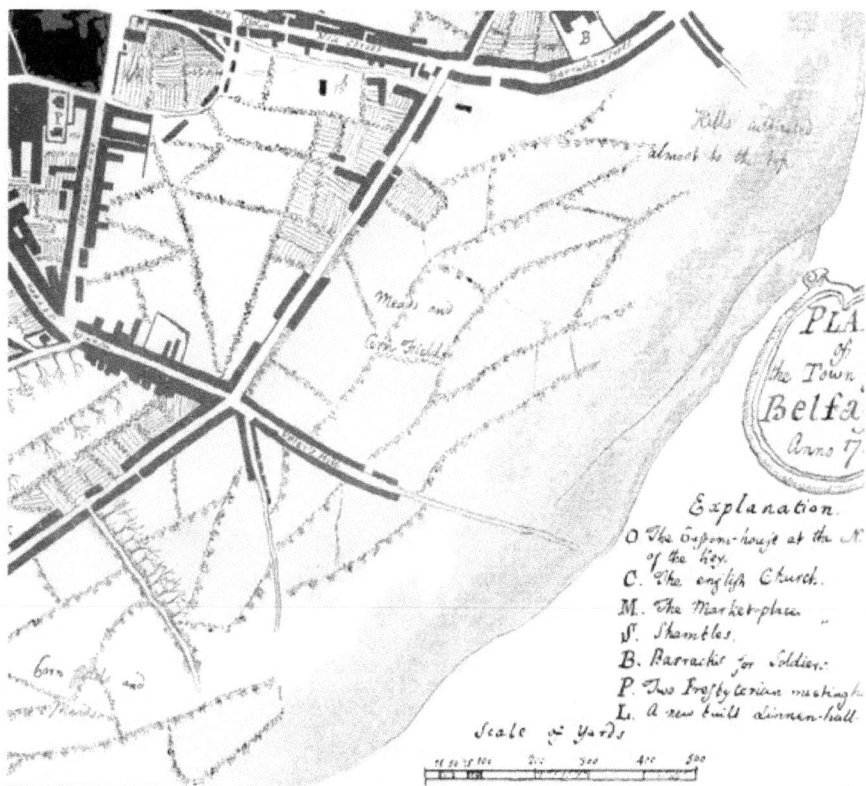

PLA
of
the Town
Belfa
Anno 7

Hills cultivated almost to the top

Mears and Corn Fields

STREET

Corn Fields and

Explanation

O. The Custom-house at the N
of the Key.
C. The english Church.
M. The Market-place.
S. Shambles.
B. Barracks for Soldiers.
P. Two Presbyterian meeting-ho
L. A new built Linnen-hall.

Scale of Yards

25 50 75 100   200   300   400   500

Population, 8,549.

in Dublin, and now for the first time published,
s M Ewart, Esq.

Appendix G.

BELFAST LIBRARY

AND

SOCIETY FOR PROMOTING KNOWLEDGE.

Laws of the Society.

I.

Object of the Society.—The object of the Society is to promote knowledge by the establishment and maintenance of a Library, and by such other means as the Society may from time to time deem it advisable to adopt.

II.

Constituents of the Society.—The Society consists of Proprietors and Members, duly admitted and qualified in the manner hereinafter stated, and none others are competent to vote at any of its meetings, or to fill any office in its management. Annual Subscribers are, however, admissible to the use of the Library, under the rules and regulations hereinafter contained.

III.

Proprietors by Election.—Every candidate for election as a Proprietor must be recommended as a fit and proper person for admission into the Society by a Proprietor or Member, in a printed form to be prepared for the purpose by the Committee. The name of each candidate shall be notified in the circular summoning the next meeting of Committee, at which he shall be balloted for ; the admission fee of Two Guineas, together with whatever proportion of the annual contribution of One Guinea may be payable on account of the unexpired part of the current year, having been previously paid. A majority of the members of Committee present shall be competent to admit.

IV.

Proprietors by Transfer or Bequest.—Any Proprietor may, by writing, under his hand, addressed to the President or Secretary, transfer his interest in the Society, or may bequeath it by Will; but the eligibility of the Assignee or Legatee shall be determined by the Committee in the ordinary mode of election. If duly elected, such Assignee or Legatee shall become a Proprietor without payment of any further admission fee, but shall be liable for arrears of subscription. If rejected by the Committee, the Proprietor, or his legal representative, shall have the power of nominating others, until a person be named who shall obtain the majority of votes.

V.

Annual Contribution Payable by Proprietors.—Each Proprietor shall contribute to the Funds of the Society One Guinea per annum, payable in advance, and falling due on the first day of January in each year. No Proprietor, whose annual contribution is unpaid, can vote at any meeting of the Society, or hold any office. Every Proprietor, whose annual contribution is twelve months in arrear, shall receive notice of his default through the Post Office or otherwise, and unless such arrear be paid off within two months from the receipt of such notice, he shall cease to be a Proprietor.

VI.

Members.—Whereas, by a law passed in the year 1843. it was enacted that persons might be admitted under the designation of " Members," who, after election by ballot in the same manner as Proprietors, and on payment of an admission fee of 21s., and an annual subscription of One Guinea, shall be entitled to all the rights and privileges of Proprietors, except the power of transferring or bequeathing their interest in the Society, it is hereby provided that Members shall enjoy the above rights so long as their annual subscription is continued. Members may at any time become Proprietors on payment of One Guinea as an addition to their former admission fee, without being proposed or balloted for a second time. Any Member duly elected may compound for his annual subscription by the payment of Eleven Guineas in one sum.

VII.

Annual Subscribers of One Guinea.—Persons desirous of the privilege of using the Library, without becoming Proprietors or Members, may be admitted as Annual Subscribers of One Guinea, by the Committee, on being recommended and balloted for, as in the case of Proprietors by election ; one year's subscription having been previously paid in advance, together with the proportion of the annual subscription that may be payable on account of the unexpired part of the current year. They shall be entitled to have two volumes at one time out of the Library, as stated in the Regulations, and shall have free use of the Reading-room during Library hours. They may at any time become Proprietors by paying to the Treasurer the admission fee of Two Guineas, without the necessity of being proposed or balloted for a second time, or may in like manner become Members on payment of an entrance fee of One Guinea.

VIII.

Annual Subscribers of Half-a-Guinea.—That apprentices and other young persons under 21 years of age, on a satisfactory guarantee, shall be eligible for admission to the Library, on payment of 10/6 per annum, and shall have the right to take out one book, and to read in the Library, but without other privilege. This privilege will require renewal annually. The Committee shall also have power to admit other persons under *special circumstances* to the same privilege and on the same conditions as to payment, guarantee, and renewal. This Law to take effect from 1st January, 1876, and to apply to all the present Half-guinea Subscribers, as well as to new applicants. All Half-guinea

Subscribers shall be eligible to become One Guinea Subscribers without a new ballot. [Enacted 18th November, 1875.]

IX.

Management of the Society's Business.—The Business of this Society shall be conducted by a President, Vice-President, Treasurer, Secretary, and a Committee of Eleven, under the control of the Society at Large; to be annually elected by ballot, at the General Meeting in February in each year. The President, Vice-President, Treasurer, and Secretary to be *ex-officio* members of Committee : five to form a quorum.

X.

General Meetings.—The Annual General Meeting of the Society shall be held on the third Thursday in the month of February in each year, when the Report of the Committee shall be read, and the Treasurer's account, as audited ; a new Committee shall be chosen by ballot ; an Auditor, not being a Member of Committee, shall be appointed ; and any Regulations which may be deemed necessary for the management of the Society's affairs shall be made. Special meetings shall be called by the President on receiving a requisition from five Proprietors or Members, stating the object of the proposed meeting. Three days' notice of every General Meeting, whether Annual or Special, shall be given by circular letter addressed to each Proprietor and Member, or else by advertisement in two or more newspapers published in Belfast.

XI.

Form and Manner of Voting.—All elections, whether in the Committee or by the Society, shall be by ballot, and all divisions shall be decided by the majority of qualified persons actually present and voting. In either case, the Secretary shall call over the names of the qualified voters present who have paid their subscription for the current year, and each, as his name is called, shall deposit his ballot or record his vote.

XII.

The President.—The President, or in his absence the Vice-President, or in the absence of both, a Chairman appointed by the meeting, shall preside at meetings of the Society and its Committee, with full power to preserve order in debate. In case of a division, he shall have a concurrent vote with the other members, and, if the votes be equally divided, he shall also have a decisive or casting vote. He shall cause the proceedings of each meeting to be read over at the commencement of the succeeding one, and, if found correct, shall certify them by his signature. The President, or, in case of his absence or illness, the Vice-President, shall have power to summon, at any time, an extraordinary or special meeting of the Society, in the manner elsewhere prescribed in these laws.

XIII.

The Treasurer.—The Treasurer shall receive all sums paid to the account of the Society, and make, out of the cash belonging to the Society in his hands, such payments as may be directed by the Committee, keeping an accurate account of both. He shall not issue any money on account of the Society without an order from the Committee, authenticated by the signature of the President, or the Chairman of the meeting. He shall, from time to time, keep the Committee informed of the state of the funds; and shall lay an abstract of his account, certified by the Auditor, before each annual meeting.

XIV.

The Secretary.—The Secretary shall take care that the proceedings of the Society and its Committee are correctly recorded, and that such notifications as the Society or its Committee may direct are duly sent by the Librarian to the persons to whom they are to be communicated. He shall also conduct the Society's correspondence, and shall from time to time lay before the Committee such parts thereof as may require its decision or confirmation. In case of his absence, the meeting shall appoint a Secretary *pro tempore.*

XV.

Powers and Duties of the Committee.—The Committee shall meet on the first and third Thursdays of each month, at eleven o'clock. When fewer than five members are present, the President, Vice-President, or, in their absence, the senior member present, shall invite as many of the Proprietors or members who first appear as may be necessary to form a quorum, to sit as Members of Committee for that day, provided that there be three Members of Committee present at the giving of such invitation. If a quorum of five cannot be obtained, the members attending shall have the power of passing books and lending out restricted books. The Committee shall have the power of appointing a Librarian, Sub-Librarian, and Porter, and of dismissing them when they see cause; of purchasing, or procuring on loan, books, maps, or other requisites; but it is hereby declared, in conformity with the object and uniform usage of this Society, that they have not power to purchase any novels or romances, except such as may be embodied in the collected works of their authors, or in Monthly Publications containing Essays and Papers on other subjects. They shall have the power of filling up vacancies in their own number, in the case of death, resignation, or refusal to act; and of investigating the state of the funds and other property. They shall examine new books and books lately bound, inspect the Registers, Librarian's Registers, impose fines, and make a report to the Annual Meeting. They shall have power to make any Orders and Regulations, not being inconsistent with these Rules, which they may deem necessary for the satisfactory management of the Society's business, such Orders and Regulations to be valid till the next General Meeting of the Society. And should any controversy arise in Committee as to the interpretation of these Rules and Regulations, it is hereby declared that, for the immediate guidance of the members present, such questions shall be determined by the votes of the majority in the usual way.

XVI.

The Auditor.—The Auditor shall, previously to each Annual Meeting of the Society, examine the Treasurer's account of the income and expenditure of the Society during the preceding year, ending with the 31st day of December, comparing the vouchers, and shall lay before the said meeting a correct abstract of the same, showing the balance due to or by the Society at that date.

XVII.

Expulsion of Disorderly and Refractory Proprietors, Members, &c.— Any person enjoying any privilege in connexion with the Society, who shall conduct himself in a disorderly manner at the meetings or upon the premises of the Society, or who shall persist in the violation of any of its laws or regulations, may be expelled by a General Meeting summoned specially for the purpose, provided that two-thirds of the persons present and entitled to vote at such meeting shall vote for expulsion.

XVIII.

Permanence of the Society.— The Society pledges itself to each Proprietor and Member, not to dissolve itself, or proceed to a division or dispersion of the property, without the unanimous consent of two General Meetings specially convened for the consideration of such question. This law is not to prevent the sale of duplicate or imperfect copies when authorized by the Committee.

XIX.

Enactment, Repeal, and Alteration of Laws.— A Resolution, if approved at a General Meeting, shall be valid till the next Annual Meeting of the Society; but if it be desired to enact a permanent law, or to repeal or alter a law already existing, notice of the proposed change or enactment must be hung up in the Library at least two weeks before the General Meeting at which it is to be taken into consideration. If then approved or modified, it shall be acted upon as an *ad interim* Law, but shall not become permanent until it has been approved by a second General Meeting, after the observance of the same formalities.

Regulations of the Library.

1. The Librarian shall attend in the Library every lawful day from Ten o'clock till Six; and every Monday, Wednesday, and Friday from Half-past Seven till Nine p.m., subject to any change that shall be made by order of the Committee. He shall have charge of the books and other property, for the safe keeping of which he shall be responsible. He shall hand to persons having the use of the Library such books, maps, &c., as they may wish to peruse or to inspect, and shall afterwards return them to their proper places. He shall keep a registry of the books lent out, taking care that no person shall have more than the regulated number of volumes at a time without a special order from the Committee. He shall have all books that have been inspected and approved by the Committee properly stamped before they are lent out. He shall report to the Committee all books that are detained beyond the time allowed for their perusal; all damage done to the books or other property of the Society; all subscriptions in arrear; and all fines incurred. He shall suspend the circulation of any book when it requires binding; call in books that may have been detained beyond the proper time, as limited by these rules; apprize new Proprietors, Members, Subscribers, Officers of the Society,

&c., of their election ; summon the Members of Committee to the Ordinary and Special Meetings ; and keep a register of the weather. He shall not lend out any book, &c., save to a Proprietor Member or Subscriber or to persons authorized to procure same for them.

2. No Proprietor or Member shall have the loan of more than four volumes at a time, without the permission of the Committee ; nor shall an Annual Subscriber of One Guinea have more than two volumes, nor any Half Guinea Subscriber more than one volume, without such permission. A periodical to count as a volume.

3. The time allowed for the use of an octavo, or small volume, is fourteen days ; for a quarto, thirty days ; for a folio, two months ; but at the expiration of those periods the loan may be renewed to the same applicant if no other has applied for it ; and Proprietors, Members, or Subscribers, residing four miles from Belfast, may keep a book for six days longer than the times above specified. It shall be in the power of the Committee to shorten the above periods in the case of books newly received. Any person detaining any book or books after receiving notice from the Librarian of the expiration of the time allowed for perusal, shall pay a fine of 2d. per day for each volume so detained, one day after the notice being allowed to persons within five miles of Belfast, and three for persons residing beyond that distance, for returning the books.

4. An Application Book shall be kept in the Library, in which any Proprietor, Member, or Subscriber may enter his name as applying for the loan of any book that he may wish to peruse ; and the Librarian shall send to applicants, in the order of their application, a card notifying that the book or books so applied for are ready, provided always that no person shall be allowed to have more than one work at a time of those specially applied for ; he shall not be entitled to enter his name as applying for more than two works and one periodical at a time ; nor, if he has one periodical, to enter his name for a second till he shall have returned the first ; or to have more than one periodical at once of the current month.

5. Any person entitled to take out a book may, instead, require the Librarian to keep it for such time as he would be entitled to keep it out, for the purpose of his reading it in the Library. Any book so kept out shall count as if taken out.

6. Books shall not be entered in the Catalogue, nor lent out, until inspected by the Committee or a Sub-Committee ; but, in the meantime, shall lie on the Library table for the use of the Proprietors, Members, and Subscribers. Periodicals, if published quarterly, shall not be lent out until they have remained one month in the Library ; if published once every two months, they shall remain three weeks ; if published once a month, or oftener, a fortnight.

7. A Proposal Book shall be kept in the Library, in which any Proprietor, Member, or Subscriber may enter the title, character, and price of such books as he wishes the Committee to order, annexing his name. These entries shall be read at the next meeting of the Committee, and the books shall be ordered or rejected at the next meeting in succession.

8. Books entered in the Catalogue marked thus (†) are never to be lent out. Books marked thus (**) to be lent out only on an order from the Committee, and on the applicant depositing with the Librarian the full value of the entire book or set of books of which it may form a part, and giving him a written acknowledgment for the same. For books marked thus (*) a receipt must be given to the Librarian. Any Member borrowing a restricted book shall be held responsible for the state in which it shall be returned by him, unless he point out to the Librarian, before taking it out of the Library, the damage which it had previously sustained. The Librarian shall examine, on its return, every restricted book that has been borrowed; and, in case of its having sustained damage while in the borrower's custody, he shall not give back the deposit until the book has been inspected by the Committee, and accepted by them.

9. A Proprietor or Member may introduce a stranger, not residing within ten miles of Belfast, or a gentleman who is only a temporary resident in the town, to read in the Library during Library hours; the introducer engaging to be responsible for his friend, and entering his name in a Visitor's Book, which shall be kept in the Library for that purpose.

10. Any Proprietor, Member, Subscriber, or Visitor injuring the property of the Society, shall make such compensation as the Committee shall determine; and any Proprietor, Member, or Subscriber lending a book the property of the Society to any person not a Proprietor, Member, or Subscriber, shall be subject to a fine of ten shillings; and if any Proprietor, Member, or Subscriber or Visitor, shall take any book out of the Library without giving notice to the Librarian, or in violation of these regulations, it shall be in the power of the Committee to refuse to the person so offending admission into the Library until he has paid such fine as the Committee may impose upon him, and has entered into an engagement not to infringe the rules in future.

Appendix H.

Subscribers to the Library, 1887-8.[1]

Proprietors, 64.

Anderson, John, J.P., F.G.S., Holywood
Andrews, Mrs., Comber
Andrews, Miss Elizabeth, College Gardens
Armor, John, Drumbeg
Barnett, Dr. J. Milford, College Gardens
Barron, George, Dunluce Street
Bell, E. H., Linen Hall
Bellis, George, J.P., Ballymena
Bowman, Davys, 14, Elmwood Avenue
Bristow, Miss, Dunmurry
Browne, Dr. S., R.N., J.P., College Square
Brown, John, Bedford Street
Bruce, Miss, The Farm, Antrim Road
Bryce, Rev. Dr. R. J., Fitzroy Avenue
Burden, Dr. Henry, Alfred Street
Clarke, Edward H., Queen's Elms
Connor, Charles C., Linen Hall
Dill, Dr. Robert F., Fisherwick Place
Dill, Samuel, Knock
Drennan, Dr. J. S., Prospect Terrace
Ewart, Sir Wm., Bart., M.P., Bedford Street
Ferguson, Miss, Wellesley Avenue
Fullerton, Robert F., Donegall Place
Gordon, Robert A., J.P., Summerfield
Gordon, Robert W., Upper Falls Mills
Grattan, Miss, Fortwilliam
Greer, Thomas, J.P., Seapark
Greer, Frederick, Tullylagan, Dungannon
Grimshaw, O'Donnell, Castle Street
Harkness, James, Cultra
Hodges, Dr. J. F., J.P., Windsor
Ireland, Miss J., Holywood
Jackson, A. T., C.E., 5, Corn Market

Kelly, H. C., Greenisland (Life Member)
Kennedy, Miss, Clonard
Keown, Thomas H., Sydenham
L'Estrange, Thomas, Howard Street
Lindsay, Mrs. Robert, Malone
MacAdam, Robert, College Square East
Murray, Mrs. G., Sydenham
M'Clure, Sir Thomas, Bart., J.P., D.L., &c.,
    Belmont
O'Neill, James, M.A., College Square East
Parker, Dr. H. R., Methodist College
Patterson, E. F., Corporation Street
Patterson, W. H., M.R.I.A., High Street
Porter, Miss M. E., Botanic Avenue
Porter, Hugh, Alexandra Villas
Reid, Mrs. Henry, College Gardens
Ritchie, —, Ballymacarrett
Robinson, W. A., J.P., Cultra
Shillington, J. J., J.P., Glenmahon Towers,
    Strandtown
Simms, F. B., Linen Hall
Smyth, Miss Eliza, Williams' Place
Smythe, Rev. G. C., Carnmoney
Suffern, John, Windsor
Swanston, William, F.G.S., Cliftonville
Thomson, James, J.P., Macedon
Tilley, James, Botanic View
Walkington, D. B., Thornhill
Ward, Isaac W., Linen Hall
Weir, John, Bangor
Workman, Mrs. Robert, Windsor
Workman, William, Nottinghill
Workman, Rev. Robert, Newtownbreda

(1). An asterisk prefixed denotes election in 1888.

Members, 199.

Abbott, John, Botanic Avenue
Aicken, Dr. Wm., Murray's Terrace
Alexander, D. B., Carrickfergus
Allen, David, Princess Gardens
Anderson, Mrs. D., Cookstown
Andrews, Mrs. Thomas, College Gardens
Andrews, Mrs. W., Victoria Place
Andrews, Samuel, J.P., Seaview
Arbuthnot, W. H., Royal Avenue
Arnold, Mrs. J. A., University Square
Arnold, Dr. Wilberforce, J.P., Crescent House
Atkinson, J. H., College Gardens
Atkinson, C. R., Windsor
Bailey, Dr., Cliftonville
Barbour, James, J.P., Holywood
*Barkley, Dr. G., Maghera
Barr, James, Sandringham
Beatty, Thomas, Newtownards
Bell, William, J.P., Silverstream House
Bibby, Rev. J. H., Downpatrick
Bigger, Rev. Professor, Magee College, Derry
Black, Mrs., College Gardens
Black, Samuel, J.P., Drumnaul House, Randalstown
Boyd, S. B., Castle Place
Braddell, Edward, Malone Road
Brett, C. H., Fortwilliam
Brett, John H., County Court House
Browne, William, Cookstown
Bulloch, Alexander, Linenhall Street
Busby, Rev. Dr., University Square
Campbell, Hugh, Waring Street
Campbell, John, Rathfern, Whiteabbey
Campbell, William, Bismarck Street
Carmichael, Mrs. D., Donaghadee
Carmichael, Mrs. W., College Green
Carson, Thomas G., Coleraine
Carson, Mrs., Coleraine

Carson, William, J.P., Royal Avenue
Charley, Mrs. John, Wilmont Terrace
Child, Alexander, Botanic Avenue
Coates, Foster, Derryvolgie Avenue
Corry, Sir J. P., Bart., J.P., M.P., Dunraven, Malone
Cowper, Mrs., Agincourt Terrace
*Cowper, Rev. G. T., Rathfriland
Craig, H. C., Mountcharles
Crawford, George, Banbridge
Crawford, William, Callender Street
Cuming, Dr. James, Wellington Place
Cunningham, Josias, Waring Street
Cunningham, Mrs. W. C., Fortwilliam
Davis, Rev. John, Ballynahinch
Deacon, Mrs., Antrim Road
Deacon, Rev. J. J., Clough
Dods, Robert, Dunluce Street
Dorman, Robert, Linen Hall
Dunkerley, Rev. Thomas, Comber
Everett, Professor, Princess Gardens
Ewart, William Q., Bedford Street
Ferguson, John, Rugby Road
Ferguson, J. H., Knock
Finlay, W. L., J.P., Royal Avenue
Gallaher, Mrs. R. M., Greencastle
Gamble, Mrs., Royal Terrace
Geddis, Colonel, Cliftonville
Glover, John, Montpelier, Malone
Gordon, John, College Park
Gordon, Rev. Alexander, Upper Crescent
Gordon, Dr. William, J.P., Saintfield
Gowan, Henry, Greenwood
Greene, Rev. J. P., Queen Street
Gregg, Henry, Sydenham Avenue
Gregg, William, Strandtown
Grimshaw, N. W., J.P., Dunmurry
Hamilton, Rev. Thomas, Brookville
Hardy, Thomas L., College Street South

Members.—*(Continued.)*

Harbison, M., Ravenhill Terrace
Henry, W. T., C.E., Hillsborough
Herdman, Mrs. John, 6, College Square
Herdman, F., Lisburn
Hoey, Mrs., Windsor
Howard, J. J., Mount Pleasant
Inglis, James, Abbeyville, Whiteabbey
Inglis, Mrs.,   do.   do
Ireland, A. L., Ulsterville Avenue
Irwin, Rev. John, Strabane
Jamieson, Doctor, Newtownards
Jamieson, Robert, Strandtown
Johns, Mrs. Digby, Carrickfergus
Kamcke, Wm. R., Linen Hall
Keegan, John J., J.P., High Street
Kelly, Mrs., Clonsilla
Kertland, E. H., Edenderry
Kidd, George, Dunmurry
Killen, Rev. Dr., College Park
Kinahan, Frederick, Low-wood
Kinahan, Miss, Wellington Park
Kinghan, Rev. John, Institution for Deaf
    and Dumb
Kyle, Miss R. A., Richmond
Lamb, Miss, Divis View
Lamb, W. W., Chichester Park
Leitch, Rev. Professor M., College Park
Lemon, A. D., J.P., Edgecumbe, Strand-
    town
Lindsay, —, Tyrone House
Lockwood, F. W., C.E., Royal Avenue
*Love, Rev. George C., Killeter, Tyrone
Lowry, John, Killinchy
Lowry, Mrs. John, Knock
Lytle, D. B., J.P., Bloomfield House
Lytle, Joseph H., J.P., Windsor
MacDermott, Rev. J., Belmont
MacGeagh, Robert, J.P., College Park
MacIlwaine, John H., Sydenham Park
Mackeown, S. S., Gamble Street
Mackintosh, Patrick, J.P., Newtownards

Macrory, Mrs., Ela, Antrim Road
Martin, Rev. J. D., Banbridge
Martin, Rev. James, Richmond
Martin, Rev. Professor W. Tod, Richmond
Meenan, Alexander, Belgravia
Mitchell, W. C., J.P., Tomb Street
Montgomery, H. H., Royal Avenue
Montgomery, Thomas, J.P., Ballydrain
Mullan, Mrs. William, Marlborough Park
Mulligan, Miss, Breadalbane Place
Murphy, Joseph J., F.G.S., Osborne Park
Murphy, Rev. Dr., College Park
Murray, John, Newtownards
Murray, R. W., J.P., Fortwilliam
Musgrave, James, J.P., Drumglass House
M'Cance, Colonel, J.P., Clifton, Strand-
    town
M'Caw, George C., Elmwood Avenue
M'Cleave, G. W., Castle Place
M'Cullagh, —, Cliftonville Avenue
M'Ervel, E. J., 31, Rugby Road
M'Glade, F., Liscard Terrace
M'Kean, Rev. W., Strandtown
M'Robert, John, Listooder, Co. Down
M'Tear, Miss F., Richmond
Nicholson, H. J., Windsor
Nixon, Randal, Malone Road
Oakman, Nicholas, Prospect Terrace
Orr, Rev. R. H., Killinchy
Owens, Graham L., Henry Street
O'Brien, George, Franklin Street
O'Leary, Michael, Belgrave Avenue
Park, Professor, Mountcharles
Park, Rev. William, Fortwilliam
Patterson, W. R., College Park
Payne, Rev. G. T., Drumbeg, Lisburn
Pirrie, Miss, Fisherwick Place
Pollard, Matthew, Clifton Park Avenue
Price, J. C., D.L., J.P., Saintfield
Pring, Richard C., Fortwilliam Park
Radley, Joseph, Lisburn

Members.—*(Continued.)*

Reynolds, Mrs. A., The Mount, Mount-pottinger
Robinson, Rev. Prof., Assembly's College
Rodgers, John, Windsor Avenue
Rusk, John, Cultra
Scott, Rev. Charles, Antrim Road
Shaw, Mrs. C. W., Craigavad
Shaw, John G., High Street
Shaw, Rev. George, Wellington Park
Sheldon, Dr., Academical Institution, College Square
Shemeld, Albert, Portadown
Simonton, Robert, Comber
Sinclair, Miss, Dunmurry
Sinclair, Thomas, J.P., Hopefield
Smith, T. B., Clifton, Bangor
Smyth, Walter, Holywood
Stanfield, Thomas, Newington Terrace
Steen, Dr. Robert, Academical Institution, College Square
Sterling, Thomas H., Rugby Road
Stewart, James, sen., Wellington Place
Strain, Rev. Dr. J. K., Dromore
Street, Rev. J. C., Ulsterville Avenue

Tate, Alexander, C.E., Longwood
Tate, Mrs. Leslie, Lisburn
Taylor, Sir David, J.P., Windsor
Taylor, J. A., J.P., Drum House
Thomson, Miss, Fountainville
Thompson, William, Windsor
Torbitt, James, North Street
Vogan, John, Royal Terrace
Wallace, Rev. Robert, Moneymore
Ward, John, J.P., Lennoxvale
Weir, Miss, Bangor
Weir, John M., J.P., 40, Clifton Park Avenue
Wilkinson, Dr. H. S., Queen's Elms
Wilson, J. K., Donegall Street
Wilson, James, B.E., Dunmurry
Wilson, Mark F., J.P., Carnlough
Workman, Dr. Charles, Belmont Terrace
Workman, John, J.P., Windsor
Workman, Rev. Robert, Kirkcubbin
Workman, Thomas, J.P., Bedford Street
Wright, Joseph, F.G.S., Donegall Street
Young, Robert, C.E., Donegall Square
Young, Samuel, Derryvolgie
Young, W. R., Galgorm Castle

Guinea Subscribers, 555.

Acheson, D., J.P., Castlecaulfield
Agnew, Henry, Malone Park
Aicken, J. B., Belgravia
Alison, Captain, Fortwilliam Park
*Allardice, Mrs. James, Knock Cottage
Allen, Mrs., Alberta Terrace
Anderson, F., 8, The Mount, Mountpottinger
Anderson, Thomas, Clifton Park Avenue
Andrews, John, J.P., Comber
Andrews, John, jun., Knock
Andrews, Michael, University Square
Armstrong, Mrs., Wellington Park
Arnold, Edgar, Marino, Holywood
*Audain, Colonel, Lower Crescent

Bailey, J. L., J.P., Mountcharles
Bain, J. F. H., Greenisland
*Ball, Townley, D.L., Antrim
*Barbour, Mrs., College Gardens
Barnett, Mrs. C. W., Bedford Street
Barnett, Dr. Richard, Wellington Place
Barron, Rev. Robert, Whitehouse
Batt, William, C.E., Garfield Chambers
*Beatty, Robert Allen, 78, University Square
Bell, Mrs. C., Balmoral
Bell, A. L., Elmwood Terrace
Bell, Charles, Crumlin Terrace
Bell, John, Linen Hall
Bell, Joseph, Whitehouse

Guinea Subscribers.—*(Continued.)*

*Beatty, James B., Holywood
Beatty, Thomas, 52, Fitzroy Avenue
Benson, George, Windsor
*Berwick, Walter, Linen Hall
Bigger, Francis Joseph, Ardrie, Antrim Road
Bigger, Miss, Clifton Park
Bingham, Rev. J., Knock
Black, Dr., Royal Terrace
Black, James, Arthur Square
Black, Mrs., Comber
Blackwood, Mrs. O'Reilly, West Elmwood
Blow, James, Donegall Square West
Boas, Hermann, Lennoxvale
Bottomley, H. H., Rugby Road
Boucher, Miss M. E., Cliftonville Avenue
Boucher, W. J., Upper Crescent
Bowles, Charles, J.P., Linen Hall
Boyd, T. B., Clifton Park
Brandon, Hugh, 51, Atlantic Avenue
*Breaky, Alexander, 4, Waring Street
Bristow, Rev. John, St. James' Parsonage
Brown, G. B., Dunluce Terrace
Brown, G. H., Clandeboye
Brown, James, Wilmont Place
Brown, J., Castleton Terrace
Brown, J. B., Limestone Road
Brown, Miss, Windsor Avenue
Brydon, W. W., Waring Street
Butchard, Mrs., Lawrington
'Calder, J. M., Bedford Street
*Caldwell, Mrs., Lismoyne, Dunmurry
Caldwell, Miss, Laburnum Terrace
Caldwell, William, Elmwood Avenue
Calwell, Alex. M'D., College Square North
Cameron, Robert, Clifton Park Avenue
Campbell, Henry, Craigavad
Campbell, John, Lennoxvale
Campbell, Miss, Windsor
Campbell, Rev. Robert, Wellington Park
Campbell, William M., Brook Crescent
Carson, Miss, Mountpottinger

Chancellor, Rev. J. A., Cromwell Road
Charley, P. H., Hopefield Avenue
Chartres, J. S., Methodist College
Chestnutt, Miss, Lisanore House
Churchill, W. G., Castle Place
*Clark, Alexander, Upperlands, Derry
*Clark, Dr., Dunmurry
Clarke, Joseph, Elmwood Avenue
Clarke, Mrs. E., Donegall Pass
*Clarke, Major-General Wiseman, Ulster Club
Clendinning, T. W., Richmond Terrace
Coakley, Frederick, Holywood
Coates, A. H., Bangor
Coates, W. T., 92, Richmond Terrace
Coe, Miss G. H., Donegall Place
Collier, Dr. W. F., Belfast Academy
Compton, G., Knock
Conland, Joseph, Alfred Street
Cooper, Rev. R. H. S., 7, Botanic Avenue
Corbett, David, J.P., College Park
*Cornish, Mrs., Llandaff Villas, Strandtown
Corry, Robert, Connaught Terrace
Corry, W. F. C. S., Ormeau Terrace
Cosgrove, Henry, Rugby Road
Costello, Rev. J. E., Whitehouse
Coulter, G. B., Donegall Place
Craig, J. H., 51, Atlantic Avenue
Craig, Mrs., Bank of Ireland
Craig, Mrs., Craigavon
*Crawford, Miss, Seaview, Whiteabbey
Cronhelm, H. C., Lombard Street
*Crowe, G. W., University Street
Culverwell, G. P., Granville Villas
*Cunningham, Miss, 14, Claremont Terrace
Cunningham, Thomas, Clonsilla
Currell, Miss, Whitehouse
Currell, Andrew, J.P., Ballygavny, Ballymena
Currie, William, Pine Street
D'Arcy, Rev. C. F., 5, Ulster Terrace
Darbishire, Herbert, Belgravia
Darley, Rev. W. S., University Square

Guinea Subscribers.—*(Continued.)*

Davidson, D. V., Royal Avenue
Davis, Henry, Holywood
Davis, William, College Gardens
Davison, Miss M., Hughenden Terrace
Despard, F. G., 151, Ormeau Road
Despard, V. D., Academy Street
Dickey, Dr. Samuel, Clifton Street
Dickson, Hugh, Belmont
Dickson, James, Fortwilliam Park
Dickson, John, Dunluce Terrace
Dickson, Mrs., Mount Pleasant
Dixon, Wakefield H., Cliftonville
Donald, Rev. Dr., Clifton Park Avenue
Donnan, Mrs., Clifton Park
Doran, J. A., Botanic View
Douglas, John, Elmwood Avenue
Dudley, Rev. F., Drumbo Rectory
Dudley-Jans, Rev. F. S., Glenarm
*Duffield, Miss M., Windsor Park
Duffin, Mrs., The Lodge, Strandtown
*Duffin, Mrs. Charles, Danesfort
Dugan, J. J., Claremont Terrace
Duncan, T. K., Botanic Terrace
Dyer, Miss, Lucyville, Whitehouse
*Eaken, W. D., Holborn Terrace
Eaton, Miss, Maybrook, Lisburn
Edgar, Mrs., Mountpottinger
*Eken, Rev. E., Dromore
Elcock, Charles, Hughenden Terrace
Elliott, Miss, Trinity Street
Emerson, Mrs., Ballysillan
English, James, Hollymount
Entrican, J., M.A., 3, Eglinton Terrace
Entwistle, James, Aspen Villas, Sydenham
Erskine, H. M., Rugby Terrace
*Evans, Silas, 2, Upper Crescent
Ewart, L. M., J.P., Bedford Street
*Ewing, Mrs., Glendhu
Fagan, Dr., J.P., Glengall Place
Faren, Joseph, Mountcharles
Fennell, W. J., Chichester Street

Fenton, F. G., Linen Hall
Fenton, S. G., J.P., Linen Hall
Ferguson, Dr., Fisherwick Place
Ferguson, Mrs., College Gardens
Ferrar, A. M., Windsor
*Ferrar, L., 4, University Square
Ferrar, Miss, Camden Street
Festu, Jules, Upper Crescent
Fforde, Miss, Grosvenor Street
Fiddis, Alexander, College Park East
Figgis, Frank F., 19, Waring Street
Filson, Mrs., Castleton Terrace
Firth, Joseph, New Barnsley
Fitzgerald, Professor, Botanic Avenue
*Fitzsimons, William, 101, Donegall Street
Flanery, A. J., Holywood
Floyd, Mrs., Donegall Pass
Fordyce, Rev. J., Lonsdale Terrace
Fraser, Thomas, Wellington Park
*Fulton, John, 22, College Gardens
Futtit, Miss, Bangor
Gaffikin, Thomas, J.P., Fitzwilliam Street
Gardner, Mrs. Archibald, Craigavad
Gardiner, Joseph, 4, Bedford Street
Gay, Mrs., Waverley Terrace
Geoghegan, Mrs., Royal Terrace
*Gibson, George, 4, Linenhall Street
Gibson, Miss, Fortwilliam Terrace
*Gilbert, Mrs., 16, Abercorn Terrace
Gilbert, William, Windsor
*Gilmore, J. A., Pakenham Place
*Girdwood, J. K., Oldpark
Glass, James, J.P., Bedford Street
Godfrey, Mrs., University Square
Godfrey, Miss, Botanic Avenue
Godwin, William, Queen Street
Gordon, George, Strandtown
Gorman, W. T., Methodist College
Gourley, James, J.P., Derryboy Cottage,
    Killyleagh
Graham, Dr. J., Donegall Pass

Guinea Subscribers.—*(Continued.)*

*Graham, Jackson, Derryvolgie Avenue
Graham, Miss, Botanic Avenue
Graham, Rev. F. M., College Gardens
Greenlees, Rev. J., Brookville Avenue
Greer, William, Rugby Road
*Greeves, Joseph, Glenside, Strandtown
Gregg, A., Willowbank
Grogan, Miss, College Gardens
*Grose, Surgeon-Major, Richmond Terrace
Grundler, E., Bedford Street
Gunning, F. P., Greenisland
Guthrie, Miss, Dunluce Street
Guthrie, William, Rosemary Street
Haddock, C. D., Wellington Place
Haines, T. C., Ulsterville Avenue
Hamilton, Rev. G., St. Matthew's Parsonage
Hamilton, Rev. H. M'C., Templepatrick
Hamilton, James, Whiteabbey
*Hamilton, R. L., J.P., Lismore, Windsor Avenue
Hamilton, Rev. T. R., Sydenham Park
Hanna, Miss L., Somerset Place
Hanna, J. C., Queen Street
Hannay, Rev. Dr., Malone
Harbison, Adam, Grosvenor Street
Harding, Rev. C. W., Ligoniel
Hardy, Miss, Fitzroy Avenue
Harper, William, Donegall Street
Harvey, William, University Street
*Haslett, Miss, 13, Upper Crescent
Hasse, Rev. Leonard, Gracehill, Ballymena
Hazleton, W. D., Brookville
Henderson, Miss, Windsor Terrace
Henderson, Mrs., Ulster Terrace
Henderson, James, M.A., Donegall Street
Henry, S. D., Wellesley Avenue
Herdman, Arthur, Ulsterville Avenue
Herdman, Henry, Royal Avenue
Herd, St. John, Linen Hall
Heron, John, Holywood

Heron, F. A., Cultra
Heron, Miss, Lower Crescent
Hetherington, Mrs., Windsor
Higgin, Wm., Rosganna, Carrickfergus
Hill, E. D., Northern Bank
Hodges, J. F. W., J.P., Craigavad
Hodson, Mrs., Lisburn
Horner, George, J.P., Cliftonville.
Houston, James, 5, Eglantine Avenue
*Houston, Miss, Fortwilliam Terrace
Houston, M. H., Fairview Villa, Ravenscroft Road
Hughes, Edwin, Newtownbreda
Hughes, Rev. George, Newtownards
Hunter, Rev. C. W., Holborn Terrace, Coleraine
Hunter, John, Ardmore, Holywood
Hunter, Miss, Belgravia Terrace
Hutton, A. W., Chichester Street
*Inglis, Captain, C. T. Staff, Fleetwood Street
Inglis, G. F., Grenville Villas
*Irwin, William, Seaview Terrace, Sydenham
Jackman, W. J., 19, Cromwell Road
*Jackson, Rev. W. J., Duncairn
Jackson, W. J., Malone Park
*Jaffé, Alfred, J.P., Cloona, Dunmurry
*Jamieson, A., 49, Atlantic Avenue
Jamieson, Hugh, Duncairn Terrace
Jenkins, James, Knock
Jenkins, William, Windsor
Johns, Miss E., Carrickfergus
Johnston, J. H., Milton Terrace
*Johnston, John G., 35, Botanic Avenue
Johnston, P. H., Royal Avenue
Johnston, R. B., Botanic Avenue
Johnston, S. A., 31, Laburnum Terrace
Johnston, W. Sibbald, J.P., Newtownards
Jones, Frederick, Wilmont Terrace
Joynt, James L., Fitzroy Avenue
*Keightly, T. R., Fortwilliam Park
Kelly, William, Provincial Bank

Guinea Subscribers.—*(Continued).*

Kennedy, R. F., Grassmere Terrace
Kerbusch, Dr. Leo, Elmwood Avenue
Kevin, Dr., Donegall Pass
Killen, Mrs. J., University Square
Kinahan, Rev. W., Donegall Pass
King, Mrs., Cromwell Terrace
Kirker, A. M., Craigavad
Kirker, G. S., Cliftonville Avenue
Kirkpatrick, Mrs., Whiteabbey
Knox, R. Kyle, Northern Bank
Knocker, Captain, Mountcharles
Knox, Mrs., 11, Hughenden Terrace
Lanyon, Sir C., J.P., D.L., Whiteabbey
Lanyon, Mrs. H., Castleton Terrace
Lanyon, Mrs. J., Lisburn
Law, William, Kinnaird Terrace
Lawther, Mrs., Brookvale House
Lee, James, J.P., Greenisland
Legate, Theophilus, Donegall Square West
Lepper, Alfred, Smithfield Spinning Mill
Lepper, Miss, Queen's Elms
Leslie, James, Somerset Terrace
Letts, Professor, Windsor
Lewis, Edward, Royal Avenue
Lindsay, Dr. J. A., Victoria Terrace
Lindsay, Miss, York Street
*Lindsay, Miss, Dromore
*Long, William, Willowmount, Cliftonville
Lough, Matthew, Marlborough Park
Lowenthal, Jules, Linenhall Street
Lowry, W. O., Fleetwood Street
Lowry, John, Linen Hall
Lowson, W. B., Chichester Park
Lynd, Rev. R. J., Windsor
Lynas, William, Alexandraville
Lyons, T. S., 8, Lower Crescent
Lyons, J. B., Cavendish Terrace
Luther, Dr., University Road
Macaulay, Mrs. John, Redhall
Macauley, R. H., Wheatfield
Macfarlane, John, Windsor

Mack, Hugh, Lisburn
Mackay, J. S., Dunluce Terrace
*Mackay, Miss, 5, Wilmont Terrace
Macklin, Mrs., Lisburn
Maclean, W. G., Custom House
MacPherson, General, Fortwilliam Park
Magill, James, Donegall Place
Magill, Rev. Dr., University Square
*Maginn, Francis, Botanic Avenue
Magowan, Samuel J., Provincial Bank
Maitland, Alex. S., Woodville Terrace
Malcolm, Mrs. A. D., Hughenden Terrace
Malcolm, Bowman, Richmond Terrace
Malcolmson, Mrs. H., Holywood
Malcolmson, James, Castle Place
Malone, John, Royal Avenue
Manley, Waring, University Square
Marsh, John, St. Clair, Holywood
Martin, Rev. E. T., Donegall Pass
*Martin, Samuel, College Street
Martin, T. J., Ashley Place
Masaroon, A. R., Lodge, Strandtown
Matier, D., Eia Street
Matier, Henry, J.P., Clarence Place
Matier, Miss, Banbridge
*Mathews, Thomas, Elmwood
Medlen, S. J., Belvidere, Windsor
*Megaffin, Mrs., Lonsdale Street
Merrick, H., Victoria Place
Mervyn, Rev. George Gore, Kinnaird Street
Millen, Samuel, Ulsterville Avenue
Miller, Miss E., 14, College Green
Miller, Mrs. Joseph, Knock
Miller, Robert, Osborne Park
Miller, T. Osborne, Cliftonville Road
Miller, W. H., Bangor
Milligan, John, Castleton Terrace
Milligan, S. F., Royal Terrace
Milling, Rev. R. G., Ballynahinch
Mitchell, A. S., Eia Street
*Moore, Mrs. John, Laurington Terrace

Appendix.

Guinea Subscribers.—(Continued.)

Montgomery, Miss, Upper Crescent
*Moore, Miss M., Elmwood Avenue
*Moore, D. William, Cromwell Road
*Moore, Samuel, Howard Street
Moreland, Alexander, Carnban House, Lisburn
Moreland, J. C., Crawfordsburn
Morell, H., Botanic Avenue
Morrison, Hugh, Ligoniel
Mulholland, James, Donaghadee
Mulligan, J. F., Victoria Street
Mulligan, Samuel, Wilmont Terrace
*Mulligan, W. G., Lurgan
Munce, Mrs., Oxford Buildings
Murney, Dr. Henry, J.P., Holywood
Murphy, J. P., Kinnaird Terrace
Murray, D. A., Lombard Street
Murray, G. E., Botanic Avenue
Murray, Robert, College Street
M'Alester, Rev. C. J., Holywood
M'Bride, Thomas, Albion Place
M'Call, W. R., Derryvolgie
M'Cance, Finlay, J.P., Suffolk, Dunmurry
*M'Cann, John, College Park East
M'Cartin, Rev. Eugene, Antrim
M'Caw, L. C. D., Avoniel
M'Causland, William, Cherryvale
M'Cleery, Mrs. H., Clifton Park Avenue
M'Connell, Andrew, M.D., Great Victoria Street
M'Connell, James, Waring Street
M'Connell, —, Comber
M'Cormick, H. M'N., County Courthouse
M'Dowell, John, Landscape Terrace
M'Farland, Surgeon-Major, Lawrington
M'Ferran, John, Fortwilliam Park
M'Kean, E., 17, University Square
M'Kee, William, Fleetwood Street
M'Kenna, R. G., Old Lodge Road
M'Keown, Mrs., College Gardens
M'Kibbin, John, Sydenham

M'Kittrick, John, Castle Street
M'Lean, F. P., Derryvolgie
M'Monagle, Alexander, Office of *Witness*
M'Mordie, R. J., Lombard Street
M'Mullan, Thomas, Cnoc Alium, Malone Road
M'Neill, Daniel, Queen's Island
M'Neill, Mrs., Parkmount
M'Neill, William, Windsor
*M'Roberts, H. R., Ballynahinch
M'Tear, J. T., Castle Place
Nance, Andrew, Wellington Park
Napier, James, 9, Montgomery Street
Nash, William, Fitzroy Avenue
*Neill, Abraham, New King Street Mills
*Neill, James, Cromac Park House
Neill, J. Ross, Windsor
Neill, Miss, Greenisland
Nelson, James, Mountcharles
*Nelson, Mrs., Nottinghill
Nelson, W. R., Bedford Street
Nesbitt, Miss H. G., Richmond
Newett, B. J., Mount Lyons, Antrim Road
O'Connor, W. P., Apsley House
O'Flaherty, F. H., Dunmurry
Orr, Rev. Dr. J. H., Antrim
Orr, J. P., Linenhall Street
Orr, Rev. R. J., Queen Street
Osborne, Rev. Henry, Holywood
*Overend, Mrs., Upper Clifton, Bangor
Park, Dr. R. C., J.P., Newtownards
Paul, Mrs., Knock
Paul, Thomas, J.P., Cliftonville
Payne, J. C. C., Botanic Avenue
Pender, Mrs., Whitewell
Pettigrew, Robert, Bedford Street
Pim, E. W., High Street
Pooler, Rev. L. A., Garfield Terrace
Porter, Mrs. R., Fortwilliam
*Powell, A. M., 62, Cromwell Road
*Price, W. G., Great Victoria Street

Guinea Subscribers.—*(Continued.)*

Pullman, J. L., Albertbridge Road
Purcell, R. D., Whitehouse
Purdon, Mrs. Charles, Antrim Road
Quinn, J. J., 19, Pakenham Street
Quinn, Miss, Richmond Crescent
Ramsay, Sinclair, Donegall Street
Ramsay, Miss, Newtownards
Rea, Dr., Great Victoria Street
Reade, R. H., J.P., Dunmurry
Reade, J. T., Donegall Square
Reid, Miss A., Parkville, Sydenham
Reid, Mrs. D. A., Belgravia
Reid, Mrs., Wellington Park
Reid, Joseph, Elmwood Avenue
Reeves, Right Rev. W., Bishop of Down
and Connor and Dromore
Rice, Mrs., Whitehouse
Richardson, E. V., Dunmurry
Richter, H. O., Strandtown
*Riddell, Rev. E. P., Cromwell Road
Riddell, Miss, Beechmount
Ritchie, John, Ulsterville
*Robertson, William, Cavehill Road
*Robinson, Mrs. E. A., Cultra
Robson, Miss, Alberta Terrace
Rodgers, William, Grosvenor Street
Roe, Rev. Dr., Belville, Ballymacarrett
Rogers, John, Queen's Square
Roper, W. H., Donegall Square South
*Rowan, C. B., 10, Connaught Terrace
Ryan, Mrs., 4, Richmond Terrace
Saunders, Mrs., Shamrock Vale, Lisburn
Savage, John, Eia Street
Scott, R. T., Richmond Place
Seaver, Ven. Archdeacon, D.D., Botanic
Avenue
Shaw, Mrs. A. M., Wilmont Terrace
Shean, William, Comber
Shillington, James, Thorndale Avenue
Shillington, Thomas F., Dromart, Antrim
Road

Simms, Miss, University Terrace
Simms, W. H., Newtownards
*Simpson, John, May Street
Simpson, W. T., Donegall Street
Sinclair, Dr. E. M., Chichester Park
*Sinclair, Miss E., Lansdowne Terrace
Sinclair, Dr. Thomas, Howard Street
Sinclaire, Miss M., Botanic Avenue
Sinclaire, Richard, Andersonstown
Smith, F. W., Donegall Square East
Smith, Dr. James, Glengall Place
Smyth, William M., Hughenden Terrace
Spedding, Dr., Antrim Road
Spiller, D. F., Marlborough Park
Stannus, A. C., Chichester Street
*Steen, Mrs. John, College Gardens
Steen, William, Fitzroy Avenue
Stelfox, Mrs., Ormeau Park
Sterling, Thomas, Windsor Park Avenue
Stevenson, John, Linenhall Street
Stevenson, Mrs., Huntley, Dunmurry
Stevenson, Samuel, C.E., Royal Avenue
Stewart, Charles, Jordanstown
Stewart, Rev. H. W., Newtownbreda
Stewart, Thomas, Thorndale Avenue
Struver, H., Callender Street
Swiney, J. H. H., Chichester Avenue
Taylor, Mrs., Strandtown
Tennent, Robert, Rush Park
Thomas, H. F., Arthur Street
Thompson, George, University Square
*Thompson, James, Donegall Square South
Thompson, John, University Street
Thompson, Major L. J., West Elmwood
Thompson, Miss, Camden Street
Thompson, Mrs., Alma Cottage
Thompson, Mrs. Hugh, Malone Road
Thompson, Mrs. John, College Green
Thompson, Mrs. Robert, Fortwilliam
Thompson, Mrs. Sarah, Botanic Avenue
Thompson, Mrs. Thomas, College Gardens

Guinea Subscribers.—*(Continued.)*

Thompson, Mrs. W., Dunmurry
Tod, Miss, Upper Crescent
Tolputt, F. S., Brookvale Avenue
Toogood, Ernst, Trevelyan Avenue
Torrens, Mrs., Rosstulla, Whiteabbey
Torrens, John, J.P., Rosstulla, Whiteabbey
Trotman, Captain, Thorndale Terrace
Trobridge, George, Mountpleasant
Turnbull, Alexander, Botanic Avenue
Valentine, George, The Moat, Strandtown
Veitel, Max, Ulsterville Avenue
Wallace, James, Clifton Park Avenue
Wallace, Miss, Albertville
Wallau, F. P., Fitzroy Avenue
Wallace, Richard, Bedford Street
Ward, J. T., Linen Hall
Ward, W. H., Wellington Park
*Walker, T. R., Rugby Road
Walkington, Miss, Sydenham
Walkington, R. B., Bedford Street
Walsh, Robert, Botanic Avenue
Wardell, Miss, Cavehill Road
Warner, Miss, Lower Crescent

*Wardell, Thomas, Newport, Hillsborough
*Watson, W. A., College Green
Webb, C. J., J.P., Randalstown
Weldon, Edward, Linen Hall
Wellwood, J. E., Knock
Wheeler, Dr., Clarendon Place
Wheeler, Walter, Lennoxvale
Whitaker, Dr. Henry, Fortwilliam Park
White, Miss, Clifton Lodge
*White, Colonel P., Royal Engineers
*White, W., The Tower, Bangor
Whitla, James A., Ben-Eden, Antrim Road
Wilson, T. H., Donegall Square West
Wilson, Walter, Ellerslie, Windsor
Wood, Miss, Alberta, Malone Road
Wood, Samuel, Donegall Place
Woodside, R. P., Queen's Square
Workman, Francis, 32, College Gardens
*Worthington, James, Hamilton Street
*Wright, Captain, Donegall Terrace
Young, Miss, Botanic Avenue
Young, Robert, jun., Holywood
Young, R. M., 7, Donegall Square

Half-Guinea Subscribers.

Almond, E. D., Fitzroy Avenue
Blackhall, W. A., 7, Donegall Square
*Brown, C. J., 9, Lincoln Avenue
*Burrows, W. B., Albany Terrace
Clough, William, Clarence Place
Kelly, T. H., Belmont Terrace, Strandtown
Kirker, Victor, Royal Avenue
Lapping, Miss, Shankhill Road
M'Daniel, Patrick, 196, York Street

M'Entee, John, Annadale Street
Phillips, J. J., Arthur Street
Russell, D., 47, Cable Street
Steele, Miss, University Street
Stewart, H., 12, Great James' Street
Studdart, Edward, Windsor Park
Taylor, Joseph, Brookville Avenue
Trobridge, H. C., Camden Street
*Whiteside, J. M., Dunmurry

An asterisk prefixed indicates the additions during 1888, and consist of 3 Members,
78 Guinea Subscribers, and 3 Half-Guinea Subscribers.

Index.

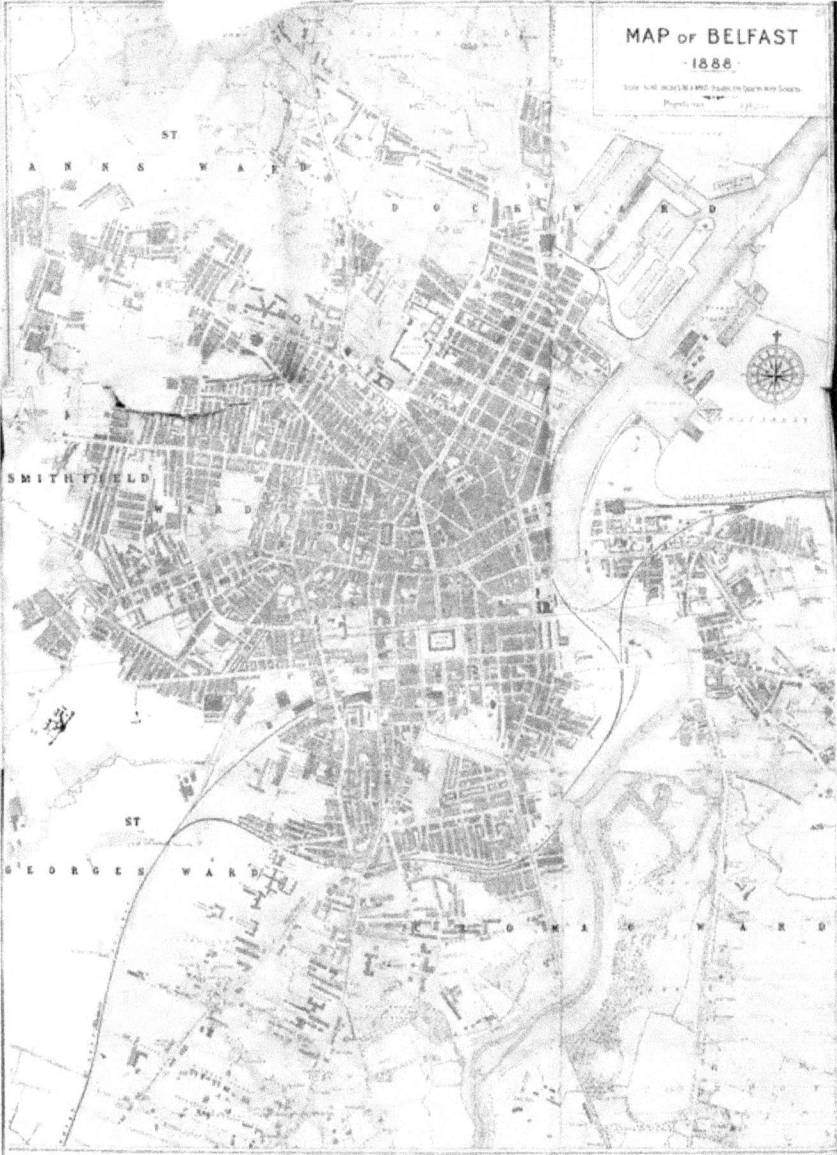

MAP of BELFAST
·1888·

ST ANNS WARD

ST

DOCK WARD

SMITHFIELD WARD

ST GEORGES WARD

THOMAS WARD

www.ingramcontent.com/pod-product-compliance
Lightning Source LLC
Chambersburg PA
CBHW020556270326
41927CB00006B/865